ELEANOR
RIGBY II

EXTRACTS FROM DIARY OF GREAT
LOVE AND LATEST COMMENTS

ELEANOR
RIGBY II

EXTRACTS FROM DIARY OF GREAT
LOVE AND LATEST COMMENTS

ZAMIR OSOROV

PARTRIDGE

A Penguin Random House Company

To order additional copies of this book, contact
Toll Free 800 101 2657 (Singapore)
Toll Free 1 800 81 7340 (Malaysia)
orders.singapore@partridgepublishing.com

www.partridgepublishing.com/singapore

"The Beatles" without alternatives

We must love and honor democracy merely for the fact that it has brought to our life just one thing only and nothing more: the willingness to respect and appreciate each other and the constant to be perfect in that art. Since democracy in modern nation states is applied on a massive scale it offers a chance to everyone, with virtually no one being left alone or cast aside from that universal democratic recovery.

The effects and positive changes associated with real democracy look marvelous and awesome - in security related matters, business and, what matters most, in our everyday life and existence. In order to achieve prosperity and success, national leaders and businessmen need to fully tap into the available potential and resources, so as to be able to provide extra services to people and community, thereby enhancing their understanding and knowledge of organizational processes, technologies, and further opportunities for innovation, inventing new things, opening new niches and possibilities.

And here is the secret why the citizens of advanced democratic countries which produce "Mercedeses", "Toyotas" and "Volvos" vehicles have not only outmatched those which manufacture the "Lada", "Moskvich", "Jiguli" and other obsolete models but why they also have a better appearance, are kind, polite and civilized compare to us. It is because, by and large, they are really better than the inhabitants of authoritarian countries.

Our oligarchs who send their children to the West are perfectly aware about these features of advanced countries. Yes, it's indeed very enjoyable to live in Finland, Sweden or Switzerland where "so many democracies and civil liberties" and what have resulted in numerous societal accomplishments, great advantages and achievements, what generates an air of politeness and kindness and feeling of protection. Therefore, when you first become acquainted with intrinsic Western values, it feels as if you have awoken in a totally different reality.

Authoritarian countries, however, have no such needs and stimulus for day by day improving their service to the benefit of their citizens. They - the authoritarian leaders and official bodies of government - have no need to be more honest, more inventive, more productive and great in the deal to showing services for the states and its prosperity.

In order to achieve personal success and advancement in life, if you happen to be born in such a country, the most important thing is to establish and maintain good terms with the governing elite. The aim is to be close as possible to the national leaders and their commands who create control and distribute the privileges, titles and honors according with own understanding and profits.

This is why the citizens of such countries - state workers, officials, public figureheads as well as cultural figures alike - look so tired, frustrated, cynical, helpless and separated from each other - because they were formed in such environment and filled with such content. Bad governance and bad principles have crushed their souls and distorted their true nature. They have never had access to the freedoms, worked with them, and they have no idea about their own possibilities, achievements and capacity to unlock their great human potential.

"The Beatles" is one of the best examples from the cultural sphere which illustrates the level of human achievement of the 20th century as well as the great possibilities offered by a free society. There have been many brilliant young men and women in the 20th century. But only the West, and more precisely the cradle and core of modern democracy – the United Kingdom - could create, nurture and support such an astonishing and heart-warming group of four young men from Liverpool. Their unique musical performances were the product of a band without any formal musical education but with the talent and strong desire to change this world with love, not through war and state power.

http://www.amazon.fr/s/ref=sr_st_relevancerank?keywords=Time+I s+Just+the+Same&qid=1407829586&rh=n%3A52042011%2Ck%3A Time+Is+Just+the+Same&__mk_fr_FR=%C3%85M%C3%85Z%C 3%95%C3%91&sort=relevancerank

http://intl-gen5.jenkins.wwe.com/connects/shop/1359712/ eleanor-rigby/

How come the West fails Big Game

(Reflection on the first visitors to Kyrgyzstan from Europe and the USA)

When the first native English speakers and new and neo colonists arrived in Kyrgyzstan and Central Asia in pursuit of their expansionist aims, they faced an entirely new situation. It was absolutely unprecedent in the history of mankind and their past experiences.

From the first day, the cultural and democratic invaders from their far away countries were fiercely attacked by all sorts of learners, teachers, students, undergraduates and postgraduates and numerous other lovers and respecters and friends of the English language.The foreigners, aliens and volunteers often felt themselves very uncomfortable from such a high level of attention to their persons.

The Kyrgyz people attacked them everywhere - at the work place and in the party, on the street, in the bus, in government buildings, outside in the open and inside the warm living room, up and down the country. It was absolutely impossible for the Westerners to escape from the good men and women, old and young, children, students, retired and full-time workers of various industries. You can't go away to countryside, on the edge of Issyk-Kul lake, or even hide yourself among mountains. Yes, Kyrgyzstan is a beautiful country with many more and much higher mountains than Scotland and even Switzerland. It seems we have plenty of space here for escaping. But you are mistaken if you thought so. Kyrgyzstan's huge mountains with its large number of locked meadow pastures have one distinct feature. Than higher you ascend, opening one by one the remotest part of them, trying advance to unknown, the greater the risk to be hunted and trapped by English learners. The people who inhabit our mountains are much more passionately greedy for foreigners, much more hospitable, energetic, healthy and curious and sincere and diligent in their intention to learn English, compared with the people who live on the foot of those mountains.

Eventually the first visitors to Kyrgyzstan must have been willing to flee and despised from inherent expansionists intentions which lived in the hearts of many generations of Englishmen. Yes, they run to their England, USA, France, Switzerland, Denmark, Germany and it seems they will never try to come to us, fearful of our unprecedented hospitality.

https://riidr.com/search/Eleanor%20Rigby/

My first love quantum dance

My first love?
Seems I couldn't remember precisely
the starting point
of such a great occasion
in my biography.

It's gone out,
hidden,
dissolved
and vanished forever
in a kaleidoscope of whirlwind
of my early recollections, visions, fantasies,
and dreams and dreams in dreams.
Or that love just playing a quantum trick with us
suggesting multiple options,
when we are with fear and surmise
coming for a great choice again?

Input, output or kaput?
The question is still open.
My first love preferred eternal dance?
How could I acted with discrepancy?

From the novel "Eleanor Rigby"

http://www.chapters.indigo.ca/home/search/?keywords=Great%20
love&langtype=4105&facetIds=528239%7C#facetIds=750051%7C
561000&page=0&priceValues%5B%5D=0&priceValues%5B%5D
=15&sc=&sf=&sortDirection=0&sortKey=Name_en

http://www.amazon.in/s/ref=nb_sb_noss_1?url=search-
alias%3Dstripbooks&field-keywords=partridge%20singapore&spr
efix=partr%2Cstripbooks

Among the grandes and the eternal blossoming of alma-mater

A book for the students - the kind of reading preferred by this group - and about students world (realities, fantasies, dreams), from various countries and times. Mercie France, for the such great respect.

I am among the Alice Munro, Le Guinn, Lyis Borgese, Washington Irving, Gogol, Tagor and others grandees.

Many authors are unknown to me yet the titles of them are clearly witnessed about the marvelous content:

14,000 Reasons to Be Happy and Other Stories (2014),
Rich Town Poor Town (2014),
The Immediacy of Emotional Kerfuffles (2013),
A Tragicomédia Acadêmica (1992),
Crystal Frontier (1998),
Water from the Moon (2002),
My Plan to Kill Henry Kissinger (2010),
Stained-Glass Elegies (1990),
A Thousand Years of Good Prayers (2006),
Lovely Delirium (2013).

http://www.amazon.fr/Students-Student-Life-Short-Stories/s?ie=UTF8&page=1&rh=n%3A83649011%2Ck%3AStudents%20%26%20Student%20Life

The application of Einstein's $E = MC^2$ equation

The more you are advancing step by step toward love, yours aim and mission, the more you are rewarded by them - they drift towards you and inspire and support your efforts.

Then once your speed is ramped up to the speed of Light (C), even more power and energy is accumulated into you - at the last instances and finishing point of distance your influence has grown exponentially and even super-exponentially - you are effectively transformed into Light and will able to create great miracles.

"Love might really be able to transform our reality and even completely undo it - to the extent that the great distances, political, cultural and others barriers have vanished and you are before me and nothing else is left in the world".

"The law of attraction applies the same principles. Than more you love somebody or something (without any difference), the more you attract it to yourself. At the highest level of self-realization you are able to perform miracles, make great discoveries, transform reality and life, capture fantastic visions and dreams".

Yes, we once witnessed such an extraordinary thing. The impressive telepathic trick performance was executed by the Jolchuby, when thanks to the great power of love he created a bridge between Kyrgyzstan and England.

'It is absolutely irrelevant what the object of your love and attraction is. Is it God in heaven with whom you want to communicate and whose attention you wish to capture or is a just beautiful creature from a far away and unknown country that once upon a time in your children years descended into your early mornings dreams in the summer house at the slope of mountain of Kyzyl-Suu and deeply your heart, stunning your imagination for the rest of your life? The law of cause and effect works correctly. What you loved, that you attracted to himself gradually and patiently and inevitable with mathematical exactitude.

Though this may sound slightly blasphemic but in fact it has nothing to do with blasphemy. God has lives within our heart and soul of everyone and expresses himself through us. And love itself is the measure of the God's presence within us".

This page also give us the proof that the equation of love suggested by Jolchuby on the basis of Einstein's physical law works correctly. The author of "Eleanor Rigby" has not such a unique combination of gifts and talents as his friend and hero of the novel Jolchuby. So he was not able to create the telepathic bridge between England and Kyrgyzstan and find his love as Jolchuby did.

But author really has in his heart the tiniest particle of true love for Western values and democracy and you see as nearly thousand people worldwide come to here each day to read what I sheared with them. It was a true miracle for me, because I know how difficult it is to for a poet and writer to attract even 50 readers.

It has happened because people really felt that this man truly has a love and belief and attracted by them. Really, I have not any other things, gifts and features even my English is rather strange, limited and oddly sounding to native English people so I have nothing what I could suggest with pride to my readers, except for the thinnest seed of love for the people from 30 countries where my book has sold, for whom who shared his love or just understand and agree with his aims and visions.

"Eleanor Rigby", Part I, XIII

...All my investigations didn't just intensify, but absorbed me totally in the explosion of hard work, which had astonished many people even before. Then it became almost monstrous, as if in me some hidden appalling forces had been awakened, forces like thermonuclear energy, whose secret rules I began to master. I understood that the power of the human mind is limitless, within a short time I apprehended the deep secrets of parapsychology, higher mathematics, the theory of light; I understood, that the theory of relativity had a much more universal character, embracing not only the physical world but also spiritual essence, the cosmos, the speed of human thinking whose efficiency is almost equal to the speed of light, we experienced the same as during physical motion at enormous speed: the world around us unravelled its secrets, and we perceived its fundaments in that flight fly further — to the most remote future and even beyond its limits, obtaining immortality directed at light. And then there's nothing impossible for us and nothing inaccessible, the most wonderful, unrealisable dream begins to unfold in reality, the most impudent gust of fantasy come true all of a sudden. That days all my life turned into continuous revelation, into a sparkling flow of inspiration, different ideas, surmises and enlightenments were trustfully surrounding me, they were crying out to be written down in my scientific notebooks and I absorbed them insatiable, enjoyed their beauty and freshness and went on taking up new ideas. It was not scientific fame or career that attracted me, all my attempts were aimed at unveiling the biggest mystery in my life.

...The distance between me and this "light", moving in fog on the bank of the river shortened steadily step by step, dream by dream.

...Little by little we were moving towards each other, and gradually some silhouette, as if under an artist's brush took a more and more distinct shape. When I approached it closer finally, the scales seemed to fall from my eyes. Remember that everything was going on in a dream which repeated itself once or twice a year and which required of me an incredible energy. The following happened all of a sudden, as always after a night of hard work. In front of my eyes appeared a smiling fascinating girl in white. Her hair was light, a little curly, thrown back by the wind, she was all light, purity and radiance, as if she was made of light, of that cloud on the bank of the river. I saw her with unusual clarity and distinctness, as if thousands of suns were illuminating our rendezvous, and recognized her at once, from the first sight, as well as she recognized me, even if we had never and nowhere met before.

But nevertheless we met, recognized each other — two little human beings, lost among millions of other destinies and people, looking for each other in an unimaginable, boundless ocean, in a cosmos of millions of other visions and dreams. Oh, we managed to perform the impossible and the cause of it were our hearts which a long time ago, since childhood, or perhaps even earlier, — we ought to ask about it professor Hawkins, working over the formula for each human life and fate, beginning from the Day of creation and till Doomsday — our hearts persistently had been paving a way through to each other, sending mysterious signals, known only to them, losing and finding again the signs, rejoicing and despairing, which at last opened our eyes to everything and let us to this rendezvous.

Yes, it was our first rendezvous in a dream, just a few moments, during which we only managed to make two or three steps along the river, hand in hand, but which threw so much light upon our lives.

I saw her against the background of her home, and she saw me against the house of my aged parents. It was the merging of our two dreams, more than that, the merging of two revelations, some dual illumination, in which relatives of both sides of the mirror were reflected: as if I saw a piece of her native England behind her, and she saw my Kysyl-Suu behind me. Thus a new reality came into being in the world of dreams, where everything was familiar to me from the cradle, and at the same time there was much unknown to me before, not at all strange, but fine and dear, as sudden and full clue of my continuous troubles, dim searches and desires.

This "illumination" was so powerful and bright, that that moment the most innermost secrets of nature seemed to lay bare before our eyes, and that very moment was as an instant of the most full and profound happiness. Behind her I saw not only her house, but also persons dear to her, relatives, I saw things which were especially dear to her, and I seemed to perceive what troubled and worried her most. The same was going on with her; as well as I did she examined carefully my background behind me. Using the language of mathematics, it was dual mutual reflection — the dream, it was redemption for my sleepless nights, agonizing doubts, searches, — a dream, which was even greater than the very reality, giving birth to it.

http://www.rakuten.com/sr/searchresults.aspx?qu=partridge+singapore&sid=3#sid=3&qu=partridge+singapore&from=6&sort=0

Океан келип конокко...

Алсыз болгон күндүн биринде,
чоң энемден сактап жүргөн таберикти,
гаухардан тизилген шурууну,
кутучадан алып, кызыл ташын жиптен суурудум
отко саламын деп.

Айткан эле чоң энем апама сырын
бул суунун түбүндө жаралган буюмдун,
жети падыша жинине тийген күнү,
небере-чеберендин бири адегенде
жете турган болсо ушундай деңгээлге,
деңиздин асыл ташын өрттөсүн-
мухит болот анда күткөн коногуң.

Мен да, апам да түшүнбөй мани-маңызын,
ал турсун унутуп да калганбыз
чоң энем дүйнөдөн кайтканда айткан кеп-насилин
мындан далай жылдар илгери.

А бирок гаухар ташынан тизилген шуруу
биздин үй-бүлөөдө болгон кымбат буюму.

Далай мезгилдер шуулдап өтүп,
нечен империялар кыйрап, нечен жаңылары түптөлүп,
адамзаттын жаңжалы түгөнбөдү, бүтпөдү.
Мына мен өзүм чоң энемдин кайткан жашына келип,
апам болсо карып араң жүрүп,
эркин Кыргызстан бойго жетип,
эки ыңкылапты башынан өткөрүп,
жүргөндө, баарыбыз козголуп,
ошол жылы күзүндө Казакстандын баш калаасында
жети падышалардын алдында туруп калып мен,
бүт дүйнөдөн келген журналисттердин катарында,
Назарбаевдин заңгыраган Ак-Сарайында
ачылды мага чоң энемдин айтканы,
түшүнө баштадым бул шуруунун жандырмагын.

Ошондон кийин катар жылдар өтүп,
элимдин шайы бөксөрүп, түгөнүп,
башкалар өлкөбүздү башкарып,
каалаган нерсени жасап жүргөнүн
сезип, көрүп дап дана

улуу падыша ажооообузду
кашык менен башка чапканда,
Март, апрель ынкылабынан кийн да,
бийлик алмашып турса да,
бүт дүйнө бизге үмүт кылса да,
шериктештерибиз кыскартып ажолорубузду
Ташкент, Москва, Минск, Астана,
өнүкпөс досторубуздун кучагынан чыгалбай,
түбөлүк алы жок болушат деп биздин падышаалар,
жаным ачып, кашайып,
Батыш Европа менен Эстеримден
биротоло ажыраймын деп сестенип,
Март, Апрель ыңкылабынын максаты
ишке ашпай артка кеткенде,
геосаясий кара күчтөрүнүн
бизди кармап тумчуктуруп неткенде,
көрүп, билип, сыздап дилимден,
Океанды чакырдым мен конокко,

калкалайын деп өзүмдү, элимди,
күйгүзүп каухардын ташын отко...

Сени жердин жети падышасы кыйнап куруттубу?
айтпадым беле, тукуму буруттун,
жети падыша каарданган күндө кайрылгын деп,
эгерде андай болбосо – каякка, абдаарып,
менин каргышыман баш калкалайсың? -

сурады менден каарду үнү бар ааламдын алпы,
кийинип карыган адамдын өң-түсүн
заматта суунун чегинде пайда болуп,
каяктан суу биздин борбоордо пайда болгонун да сезбедим,
ошол замат болуп мен делбедей,
же Океан бизге көчүп келгендей,
же мен өзүмдү Океан өзүнө тартып алдыбы,
билбейм анысын, алдыман туруп калды адамдын карысы.

- Дал ошондой, улуу урматтуум, - дедим мен ага,- таксырым,
жети падыша менен беттешүүгө алсызмын,
мен сизге кайрылбас элем, жалынып-жалбарып,
мени кыйнаган, жанымды алган жалгыз адам эмес,
бир дагы өлкө эмес - жети каардуу президенттер.
Кыргызстанды эркиндикке чыкпайсың бизсиз дегендер,
авторитаризм бийлигинде биротоло сүрсүп кеткендер,
Кыргызстанды да өзүлөр менен аңга түртөм дегендер,

17

биз менен кошо жыргаса жыргайсың,
биз жок болсок, сен дагы жок болосун, сыздайсын деп,
колу-бутубузду байлады артта калган алга баспастар.
Ошондуктан мен сизге жалынып-жалбарып,
чакырдым эле үйгө конок болуңуз деп, көрүп өзүнүз иш-жайын,
элибиздин, өлкөбүздүн абалын, дарманын.

Андай болсо, балам, түшүнүктүү деп, ун чыгарды Океан обдулуп,
ал кыймылдаганда жер солк дегенсийт айланган оогунда,
жөнү бар экен сенин мага кайрылганың.
Мени жериңе конок болуп чакырганың.
жагып калган чоң энең кыз маалында,
белекке бергем мен ага далдалчыдан сырдуу шурууну
ыйык көргөнү үчүн шаар аккан тоодогу сууну.
Эч нерсе эмес, жоготкун көнүлдүн кирин,
элиңе да катуу демди бере турган келди мезгилим.

Ушул сөздөн соң аксакал көтөрүп тулку боюн,
Океан мага аталык төктү мээрин,
эч нерседен коркпо-үркпө деп үйрөтүп,
падышаларга акыл-насаат айткандай,
ажыдаарларга акараат айткандай,
күч-кубат, айбат, акыл-эс мага берди.
«Сен үчүн - купулумда толгон-токой байлыктын баары:
тонналап катылган алтын, күмүш, бермет, каухары;
сен үчүн - тоодой толкундарды жараткан кубатым,
бүт дүйнөөнүн жүрөгүн алчу турпатым.
Сен үчүн – жер бетинин көбүн жалмаган,
жашоону койнунда жараткан
аккан, топтолгон, катылган, муздалган сууларым.
дүйнөлүк карым-катнаштын түркүгү мен,
өсүү-өнөрдүн, өнүгүүнүн түрткүчү мен».

Миңдеген булак-сууларды жандандырып,
өзү менен кошо ээрчитип алып,
басып өткөн чөлдөр гүлдөп-жайнап,
келди мага Океан падышаасы
жамгырга толгон булуттарды ташып Батыш ыраактан,
региондун өзгөртүп, жумшартып аба-ырайын,
кырк төөлөргө жүктөп деңиз түбүнөн алган белегин,
кирди борборго Океан падышаасы
шаардын фонтандары чексиз оргуштап, атып,
келди мага конок болуп Океан падышасы,
Ысык-Көлдү гавань кылды
чексиз суу менен кошо агып келген Океандын кемелери,

18

Нарын суу сактагычында атом подлодкалар пайда болду,
килейген киттер, делфиндер алар менен цирк көрсөттү,
алардын үстүндө кайкып учкан албатростор,
биздин бүркүттөр менен айтышгып жатты асманда кер-муру сөздү.
Ээси кеткен таң калган биздин эл-журтка,
эзели мындай көрүп-билбеген шумдукту,
келди мага конок болуп Океан падышасы,
бүт Евразиянын, жер жүзүнүн үшүн алып,
Кремлде, Бежинде, Лондон шаарында
зор саясий толкундар жаралып,
өкмөт түзүлүштөрү алмашып,
президенттер түш тараптан мага телефон чалып, жалынып–жалбарып,
Кыргызстан үчүн жаныбызды аябайбыз деп,
келди өлкөбүзгө конок болуп Океан падышасы,
өзү менен ээрчитип малайын, кулдарды -
жерди бийлеп турган улуу державалардын
кардуу лидерлерин, согушчандарын, жетекчи-уулдарын
баардыгын анын айтканын шамдагай аткарып,
жүгүрүп турушту алдында, бийлигин унутуп.
Кээ-бирилери Океанга жагынабыз деп,
алдынан түшүп, фонтандарга боюн таштаглы,
ойногон балдар кошо жыргашты,
суу болуп кийген кийими, костюму, галстугу, ыштаны.

- Көрдүңбү падышалардын мындай маскарадын, -
деди мага күлүп кыргыз жергесинин улуу коногу.
-Эч нерседен коркпо, чүнчүбө, - деди мага, Океан,
сенин жүрөгүңдө болом мен ар-дайым, уулум чыгаан,
кайрылган күнүңдө сага жардам кылам,
дайым эркин, кубатту, таасирдүү болсун деп сенин демиң,
улуу касиетин жоготпосун деп Манасты тааныган элиң.
Кудайдын күчүнө ээ болгон адамзаттын шерин.

Мына ошол күндөн тартып, Кыргызстандын бакты ачылды
тышкы жана ички жаман күчтөр суу толкуну менен агып, житип, басылды,
өлкөбүз Евразиянын борборуна айланды, өсүп, өнүп, көрктөнүп
Манастын доорундагыдай шаан-шөкөткө, атак-даңкка Ала-Тоонун ак-калпак эли бөлөнүп.
Кыргызстан Кудайдын пилоттук долбоору экенине адамзаттын көзү жетип
биз шериктеш өлкөлөрдү туурабай, эрчибей, тескери кетип,
шериктеш өлкөлөрү артыбыздан эрчиди, бизди туурашты аргасыздан
ал турсун бара-бара жалпы Батыш менен Чыгыш да
бизге баш ийишти, баштаган көчүбүзгө кошулду алар да.
Анткени өлкөбүздү Алла-таалам, Теңирим жалгаган
Океан Манастын руху коргоду,

ар-бир кыргыздын жүрөгүндө таап бийик ордун,
каршы туралбады бир дагы империя мындай кыргызга,
тескери журтубуз аларды баарын тынчытты тыптыйпыл,
аргасыз кылды жалпы дүйнөөнү алга жылышка.

Ode to America

America, you are really the wise nation and state
who has known from the beginning about the right way
for your citizens
and established the self-governing principles
overfilled with various richness and achievements
as the effect from the good decision and distinctness.

You more than anyone helped to suffering world.
Yes, your wealth and resources are limitless
and at the same time you are modestly looking,
your governor and millionaires
never lost their head because of their power and wealth
and your presidents never changed into bad guys, never stole the
common properties
and after resigning or - toppled
never left their countries with billions
place it - secretly in Switzerland's banks.

America, you are a really wise and good nation
that knows all the secrets of powerful and skillful government,
if yours leaders make mistakes, you quickly correct them
on the various levels of your great country.
As a result you never lost the right course
which so often happened to other unhappy countries
totally dependent from the will of their leader

that were used to do what they wanted
and forgot completely about quality service and competence,
about people's will, - fate, life and - credence
and ended badly, cursed by them and history.

So I tell you long live, America,
governed by the people since the XYIII century.
You also made mistakes and were misled by bad men
with the bad conceptions and wrong ideas,
but your nature and spirit has grown in freedom
recovered fast and found a way for goodness
more healthy and holistic
than it had been before the crisis.

That is the magic of democracies' superpower
which could not get to many others countries
that suffered mercilessly from strong leaders
for hundreds and thousands years
and proceeds to hope for
a new Big Brother and Stalin and Lenin
for the new cycle of repression, violence, murders and lethargies.

So if you want prosperity for Kyrgyzstan
be as close as possible to America,
this chap has strong immunity against slave's diseases
and you starting to be healthier and wealthier
from this good relation and friendship,

and look for one interesting feature,
all the people coming from the West resemble Americans
and they all look as Martian or people from future

often simple and honest as many good Kyrgyz
came down from the big and fresh mountains,
who also possible coming from future,
looking very simple and naïve in that cruel reality
created by communists, dictators and fundamentalists.

That's why long live, America
the greatest country
two hundred years
ruled by the invisible hand of freedom,
those people, women, children, dogs and cats
so long lived in all comforts and freedoms
that looks helplessly and hopeless
when tossed out from your great aquarium, America.

And when a man from outside comes to America
without any familiarity
with the West's achievements and beauties
he will be completely gobsmacked by what has seen.

O yes, you are really great, America,
you know how to harnessing the ruling powers
and pressing and humiliating them
for efficiency, diligence and competence
you know how to speedily change rotten governors
you constantly drifted from bad to good,
from imperfect to perfect,
and therein lies yours greatness, America.

Nay, our rulers could not reach and assess
all yours excellences and possibilities

even if you try to do all for our benefit,
supporting our independence
weighing up our geopolitics and strength
in the rotten cleptocratics frame
and nurtured us with the clean milk of honesty and justice,
alas, we could not appreciate freedom,
and get out from the prison, trap and yolk
carefully prepared by Russian dominance.

Nevertheless, the Victory in your side, America,
who knows the art of rotations of men in power
and supports human values and achievements in advance
will never been conquered
by authoritative and despotic countries.
All the outfitted and outdated models of societies
sooner or later crumbled and vanished
but even God seems to like you, America.

That's why, please, get out from power
as fast as possible
Putin, Nazarbaev, Karimov, Lukashenko,
let your people have the chance for a better life
under elected and controlled governments.

Please get out away
and stop to downgrade
so stupidly and crazily
all the states who came to power with the people desires
the Georgian, Ukrainian and Kyrgyz leaders
inspired by eternally beamed ideas of Freedom and Democracy.
Yours time has run out,

please, get out and away,
before people revolt and will do so
with much blood and sacrifice.

http://www.amazon.com/s/ref=sr_pg_3?rh=n%3A283155%2Ck%3A
partridge+singapore&page=3&sort=popularity-rank&keywords=pa
rtridge+singapore&ie=UTF8&qid=1409570608

Манас, Коран, Библия и Магна Карта

Феномен сказителей эпоса "Манас" - искусство манасчи и современной кыргызской-казахской акынской поэзии, как мне представляется, дают нам возможность понять, как, в какой примерно обстановке рождались великие откровения прошлого: как ниспадали суры Корана на безграмотного пастуха в Аравии или как плотник из Назарета мог сотворить Нагорную проповедь.

Никто не отрицает, что Коран и Библия это великие религиозные (поэтические) творения прошлого. Эпос "Манас" является произведением такого рода, более того он превосходит по объему и Коран, и Библию, и Махабхарату вместе взятые и при этом создан от начала и до конца рифмованными чеканными строками.

Мы не будем здесь говорить о литературных достоинствах той или иной книги. Важно уяснить, что и Библия, и Коран, и Манас рождались из чувства глубокой веры. И Мухамед, и Христос, и Саякбай Каралай раскрывая тайны мироздания и судьбы народов мира, в ходе импровизации или откровения, погружались в состояние глубокого транса, общаясь, как они считали, с Высшим разумом.

Христос верил, что общается с Богом и нашел поддержку и понимание у миллионов людей. Однако до сих пор нет научного подтверждения существования Высшей силы, и библейской версии теории сотворения мира. При этом Христос совершил множество чудес как: воскрешение из мертвых, превращение воды в вино, управление штормом на озере и многое другое. Но, как и чудеса предшествующих пророков, они не подкреплены научными подтверждениями и свидетельствами из независимых источников.

Мухамед верил, что архангел Гавриил велит ему писать суры Корана и что поэтому все исламское писание является вечной и высшей истиной. Однако, беспристрастная наука требует доказательств этому и не находит их, зато из столетия в столетия открывала истинную и грандиозную картину зарождения Вселенной и жизни на Земле, которая не имеет ничего общего с библейским источниками и учениями и сформировалась вопреки ним. Самым великим чудом в исламе считается сам текст Корана и вознесение пророка после его смерти на небо. Эти два чуда также не подтверждены до сих пор с научной точки зрения или хотя бы из одного независимого свидетельства. Более того, библия кыргызского народа эпос "Манас" и библия коммунистов "Капитал" заметно превосходят Коран - первая с поэтической и героической, а вторая с научно-обоснованной точек зрения и эрудицией

Что же, обратимся к Ленину, который был атеистом и не верил в библейского бога, но он тоже творил в состоянии подобного транса, одержимый идеями спасти человечество от религиозного мракобесия и навсегда покончить с эксплуататорами, освободить пролетариат от капитализма. И нашел поддержку в России и во всем мире. Самым большим его чудом является разрушение российского самодержавия и построение другой тоталитарной империи - СССР, основанного на идеях марксизма-ленинизма, которые заворожили миллионы людей на планете. Было время - в середине прошлого столетия, когда более половины жителей планеты верили в идеи коммунизма. Но от этого эти идеи не стали истинами в последней инстанции, хотя в них много умных и правильных вещей, а наоборот, они принесли неисчислимые страдания человечеству, так как оказались в своей основе антигуманными, разрушительными и демагогическими.

Гитлер тоже когда писал "Майн Кампф" в австрийской тюрьме, верил на все 100 процентов, что общается с высшими богами арийской расы и желает только счастья немецкому народу и нашел поддержку у всего народа. Но от этого его учение не стало истинным, а развязало самую ужасную войну в истории.

Вот почему, дорогие товарищи, так важно развивать искусство критического мышления и подвергать все сомнению, анализу и делать выводы только на основе причинно-следственных связей и строгих научных доказательств, а не на эмоциональных прорывах и откровениях. И не бояться задавать вопросы и опровергать авторитеты и поддерживать образование, науку и "проклятых" евреев, которые все время выдумывают все новые и новые теории, изобрели интернет, фейсбук, леп-топ и гоп-топ и закон о гомиках и демократию. И вот почему надо верить Америке и Западу, которые уважает евреев, используют их интеллект и уважают неевреев, даже если они отсталые, создают условия для их развития, уважают все религии и все ценности и которым удалось создать механизм выживания и процветания человеческого разнообразия.

Можно сказать и так, что откровения и практика отцов демократии - великих пророков Западной Европы и Северной

Америки - оказались наиболее истинными и верными и выдержавшими испытание временем. Потому что они основаны на уважении прав человека и свобод.

Значит, только Демократия является истинной верой, которая спасает нас и спасет человечество и обеспечит ему развитие во всем многообразии.

The Unified Field Theory

for all kind of religions and believers and unbelievers alike
as the recommendation for the fast achievement of peace, prosperity
and harmony

According to famous Russian writer M. Bulgakov's statement, everyone will be rewarded by the measure of his belief. More impressively about belief and its power told Jesus Christ when he turned to his followers with the sentence: If you have the tiniest particle of belief, you will do everything, tell to that great mountain move to another place and it happens immediately.

Yes, modern physics proved that such a sort of transformation and kinematic phenomenon is quite a usual and ordinary thing for our universe and realm. Not only the great mountain, the universe itself was born from one tiniest point and no one knows what will happen the next with it.

All is possible because the quintessence of belief is a love, the really creativity power in the world and universe.

Therefore, you will be rewarded according to your love. But what kind of love?

Jesus Christ gives us the answer to that question, pointing for the two most valuable and precious principles among the 10 commandments from Bible.

1. Love your God from all your heart
2. Love you close ones as yourself

The prophet completely excluded from practice the negative feelings and reactions like revenge, hatred, jealousy and even judgment. He recommended to all - love and bless your enemies, no answer and react for their evilness.

Gandhi, Tolstoy and Lennon believed these principles and lived according to them, especially in the last and most valuable period of their lives. They all agreed that the principle "an eye for eye" makes humans blind.

We must empathize for the fact that these persons also kept and respected the others commandments from Holy scripture that have significantly, maybe exceptionally valuable for modern live, like:

be among the truth searchers,
do not be the false witnesses,
be among the peacemakers.

Certainly all the honest people strongly keep the others basically norms of religion, that restricted

killing,
stealing,
and suggested to respect parents.

I focused your attention on the next commandment that restricts idolatry, admiration, worshiping something or somebody.

Christians, Muslims, Jewish and other representatives of monotheistic religions explained this commandment just from the point of their monopolistic conceptions, asking believers for the worshiping of God and no one except him.

But we have suggested the broader explanation and practical and mentally entertaining and application of this commandment.

When God or Highest intellect tell us - not make or have idols – he dose not mean just only the depictions of false gods, goddesses, arts things, pop-stars, beautiful women and many others tempting things existing in our real world. He just asked to love everyone and everything in the world and be harmonious in yours feelings, because absolutely all things and souls in the world are created by God and therefore when we love these details - we expressed love and respect to their creator.

So demand or commandment for restricting idolatry was created as a preventive measure against an excessive love and worshipping, as a really valuable advice and antidote against bad consequences in the great love. If you fell in love with somebody or something and you lost your mind and if that somebody or something did not answer you, such a form of attraction might end very badly for you or your object. And in such cases the advice and commandment about not worshipping and idolatry might be valueless as the way to return for common sense and find again you lost head.

But the commandment restricting to make idol has an absolutely universal meaning and application. Not only does it apply to precious metals, beautiful women, for the pop-stars and the stars in the sky, for the great ideas and conceptions, for the science and so on... but for the God also.

Yes, we have got to true love and respect God but never will make way for idolizing Creator and transformed ourselves for his fanatics.

It was a basic misconception of all world religious that happened from attempt to separate God from us and monopolized him for his own aims. God lives everywhere and in every one of us.

So we have to love all what you want and what touched and attracted us but no one of them we could not idolizing including your God as you appreciated Him.

Keep and stick to the basics commandments, if you want to live safe and happy and be prosperous. Love your God and close ones and yourself, love the dearest object for you as strong as possible and no one has the right to judge you for that. Even more according to measure of your love you will be rewarded. But never hate and judge and condemn the object of your deep love and obsession even if it was the dearest woman, child, if they did something that disliked and deeply hurt you. No make idol from loved one - they are all creature similar to you, sometime done the wrong things. Just love and hope for better.

The similar attitude we must keep toward object of our highest worship that have had for you the first rate value. For whom or for what you have truly believed. If you believed in God - asked himself what kind of god? Is he a Jehovah, Allah, Tengir, Votan, Krishna or someone unknown to me? In any case love him and search him but do not make idol from him, not transform himself into a fanatic for him. If you stayed on the position of agnostics or even belong to atheists you also have the most dearest things in Universe which is the object of your personal religion and worshiping. For example in the post-soviet countries many people believed and were deeply obsessed about Lenin, Marx and Stalin. Among the scientists were many people who believed in science, the universe, the highest intellect, the power of Mind. I am one of them who believed in Quantum physic. In the West and East many people believed in Democracy and Magna Charta. John Lennon believed in Yoko Ono and nothing more except her.

You might believe to yourself as for the God and you will be absolutely right, because you are also an integral part of the Universe, Love and have a right to search yourself and create miracles. But not to idolize your God – nor to idolize yourself.

In any case we must not create idols from the object of our worshiping. Even if you believed sincerely in the mind and wisdom, in quantum physics or the music of the Beatles, the poetry of Keats and Shakespeare's sonnets you must just love all of them, investigate them and penetrated them as far as possible, make great discoveries and wonders but never become blind from them, never make idols out of your worshiping items.

The nature and universe and their Creator don't like such things and sustained and help you do various miracles and achievements just when you understand that and keeping firmly commandments in such harmonious and little bit strange and oddly proportions.

Yes, really Jesus Christ, Lev Tolstoy, Mahatma Gandhi, John Lennon produced many great miracles and proceeded do that thanks to keeping great power of true love. Remember advice from the prophet, if you have in your soul tinniest seed of belief or love you able to create miracles.

If we all truly understand the deep meaning of the teachings from Christ, Gandhi, Tolstoy, Lennon – our planet will be transformed into a world of love and attraction. And no one religious, ideologies and political forces will be able to separate us and diminishing and wiped out the God and his power, belong to us as our heritage and birthright.

P.S.

Poland is one of the best example of a united nation with a strong belief in Western values. As a result it has seen great achievements during the 24 year of its independence. A similar transformation has happened in Estonia, Lithuania and Latvia. But despite our love for the West we are not worshiping and idolizing it. We must do as USA and Great Britain and many other western countries did that deeply loved democracy, Magna Carta and God but never idolized them. The similar conception belongs to modern China also after it drifted away from Communist monopolist ideology toward traditional Buddhism with harmony in its nature. We clearly see the astonishing result of a truly well-balanced and harmonious love and obsessions and belief.

God really exists and creates wonders but he is presents in every one and everywhere, loves all forms of love and attractions and hates all forms of idolatry false-witnessing and non-scientific ways of thinking and acknowledging reality.

http://www.abe.pl/en/book/9781482823578/eleanor-rigby-the-chronicles-of-great-love-and-fall-of-great-empire

Почему не срабатывают заповеди?

Мы сможем создать более или менее счастливое общество, которое будет продвигаться к процветанию, если полностью избавимся от всех идолов и заблуждений и будем следовать закону, всему самому лучшему, что накоплено человечеством в этой области.

Если будем всегда и везде:

любить бога своего всем сердцем,

любить своего ближнего как самого себя,

не убивать,

не воровать,

не лжесвидетельствовать, говорить всегда правду,

почитать отца и мать, природу, землю и все, что есть во вселенной, ибо это и есть наша мать и отец,

быть мягкими со слабыми, и сильными с сильным,

не прелюбодействовать,

не поклоняться кумирам и не сотворять их.

Это древние великие истины, хорошо известные и христианам, и мусульманам и коммунистам - они восходят корнями к Кодексу Хамураппи (Древний Шумер) и основным заветам Тенгрианства (Страна Тенгир-Тоо).

Почему же эти мудрые наставления не срабатывают сегодня и вообще, плохо срабатывали в прошлом?

Все дело в том, что они совершеают чудо, когда все соблюдаются вместе. Нельзя исключить ни один пункт из этого списка. Нельзя не воровать и в то же самое время скрывать правду и лжесвидетельствовать. Нельзя любить бога и ненавидеть своего ближнего.

Человек не может жить без веры - совершенно верно, но как быть, если твой сосед многобожник или даже совсем безбожник, а ты - монотеист?

Надо просто возлюбить своего ближнего, не требуя от него перехода в свою веру.

Особенно часто нарушается верующими и неверующими заповедь - не лжесвидетельствуй, говори всегда правду. Потому что она требует личного мужества. Если я знаю, что мир сотворен 3,7 миллиардов лет назад и что человек произошел от обезьяны, рыб, микробов в ходе эволюции и буду скрывать это, значит, буду нарушатиь заветы бога. Точно такде, если страна твоя распродается напропалую, а ты говоришь, что все идет хорошо, мы идем в светлое будущее - как может бог одобрить такое?

Еще чаще нарушается заповедь - не сотвори себе кумира.

Проблема в том, что эта и все другие заповеди имеют отношение и к богам, как мы их себе представляем. Каждый верит в своего бога и это прекрасно, но при этом он не должен делать кумира и из своего бога. В Исламе, Христанстве и Иудаизме бог поставлен вне критики и закона - и это нарушение божественных заповедей.

Из бога нельзя делать кумира, его можно только любить, даже если это Йегова или Аллах или 2 тысячи других богов на планете.

Некоторые атеисты, как, к примеру, коммунисты верили от всего сердца Ленину и Сталину - они были их богами - и, действительно, добились многого. Если бы они не сотворили кумира из своих богов, то добились намного большего и не ввергли страну в пучину бедствий.

Другие атеисты верят в науку и то же добились больших успехов. Джон Леннон верил в Йоко Оно и больше ни во что на свете и посмотрите, как многого он добился! Я по своей природе многобожник - божественное я вижу в Квантовой физике, Демократии, Кыргызских красавицах, а также в природе Кыргызстана и музыке Битлз. Но я то же стремлюсь не делать кумиров из этих своих объектов. Бог запрещает и не любит этого, когда мы теряем голову из-за любви. Мы можем только любить и стремиться добиваться своей цели, но если наш Бог не отвечает на наши чувства, как мы этого хотели бы - мы не должны терять голову. Я бы давным-давно повесился и утопился, если бы всегда следовал зову своего сердца. Правоверные мусульмане совершают роковую ошибку, когда проявляют чрезмерную любовь к Аллаху и пророку Мухамеду и пытаются завлечь других в свою веру. Аллах этого не терпит. Впрочем, террористы это люди, которые потеряли веру в любовь, предпочитая всему насилие - они лишь прикрываются именем бога, чтобы совершать преступления, перечеркивая все завповеди. И убивая, и обманывая, и лжесвидетельствуя, и прелюбодействуя. Скорее, братья мусульмане, осудите эти сатанинские действия некоторых ваших заблудших собратьев, если хотите спасти веру.

Запад в целои продвинулся так далеко в будущее именно потому, что первым осознал золотой принцип - люби своего бога, но не делай кумира из него и дай возможность другим любить своего бога, как они это понимают и заслуживают.

Можно добавить еще одну заповедь - не отрицай свободу и демократию и систему ценностей Запада.

И даже такую заповедь - не завидуй еврею, особенно если он умнее тебя. Порадуйся за него и возлюби его, ведь он пордарил тебе Интернет и Фейсбук и многое другое.

Но я боюсь, что меня поймут неправильно.

The trap of expansionistic mentality

They are so designed
that they cannot live without any territorial pretension
for another country
around them, inside, outside and far away.
It's just a matter of time
when, where and with which scale
and result starting realize the plans and dream
of the mystical Russian soul.
Geogia, Ukraine and Moldova
that is only the beginning,
after conquering them
this mystical soul will start to dream about the Baltic states, Poland,
Finland, Hungary
because she firmly believes they were part of the Russian
Federation.
But if Russia joined them that would not stopped her and not
quench her hunger,
very soon she would starting weeping and dreaming about lost
lands elsewhere
in other parts of Europe – in the Balkans, East Germany, Scotland
if the world presented her these countries,
certainly Russia would actively start colonization
what else would be left of the world after USA, UK and China.
These nations had better get away from the planet altogether,

than do such problems for mystical Russian soul.
So a final agreement on earth would be established
only under the full patronage of the Russian Federation,
when you have got it, stupid gentlemen and comrades,
from NATO, US, EU and United Nations?
Peace and total omnipresent equality
must only exist under Russian dominance and legality.

http://www.fishpond.com.au/c/Books/q/Kyrgyz?rid=1803077585&o
utprint=1&format=Hardback

The snail on the edge of razor

I have never forgotten this experiment and lesson that I had had in my school's years

One day our biologist brought to class a garden snail – picked this unpleasant small animal from the glass covered with a plastic cap

- Look children this is a helix aspersa, known commonly as garden snail, which likes our grapes and lives under their leaves and eats them, that's why it is so hated by our gardeners. But I show to you one extraordinarily capacity inherent to this creature, and maybe you have more respect it for that.

After this intriguing remark our teacher extracted from his pocket a razor. The ordinary knife-like straight razor with opening sharp and big blade. This outdated horrific means for shaving has lately been dismissed by the more safely razors with two protected edges from both side of blade. Lately have been invented the pretty single edged razor and razors with two and free edges covered with teflon and so on - absolutely safely and convenient for comfortable shaving. But in the time of my childhood the big knife like razor was totally dominated as the mean for shaving.

Our teacher opened its blade and fixed razor for its handle on laboratory's tripod with sharp and long edge turn upwar in a horizontal position.

After that teacher picked up from the glass the snail by its shell and lay it right on the sharp blade.

Mollusk saddled the blade with its body, stuck to it, immovable as if paralyzed. And no wonder, the most vulnerable part of its body has touched and hanged on the sharpest surface and platform. It seem for all of us that snail's body had been seriously wounded or even cut in two by the blade under his own weight

But in the next moment to our great amazement the snail seems come to himself and start to slowly move – right on the edge of razor, toward the wooden handle. Soon it reached the handle and climbed up for it as for the harbor of safety.

Our teacher picked up the snail and turned its body upwars to show us that it was unharmed, without any marks and cuts after such a dreadful and dangerous short trip.

-   The secret of such an unusual ability and protection are hidden in the special ointment that cover the body of snails, -our teacher told us.

-   Thanks to this, snails and slags can in fact go skiing on the edge of razors as you clearly see all now.

Now that I am grown, I know people also sometimes lived and moved on the edge of razor. The brave men and person have to do it much more often than others.

The true poets and prophets also might to get to ski on the edge of razors for the sake of a nation, country and the future. And they also have a special protective ointment calling to be honest or not be among the false witnesses.

The truth has its own protective capacity, I believe. And the existing great literature and this world itself seem like the best proof of the validitiy of this concept.

http://www.barnesandnoble.com/s/Eleanor?aref=1519&csrftoken=6 VqeJ2kLLoxmcL82u41QgtFw3bd7VOsx&dref=1%2C9&keyword= Eleanor&size=30&sort=SA&startat=61

Love and telepathy

Is it really possible to find one's love trough a telepathic dream? Yes, we are all keep up mental pressure to the dearest thing and creatures around us. If you have a strong power and love you will inevitably attract a dream and vision, existed primarily in your soul and everywhere, enliven and strengthen their fragile ephemeris substances and eventually release them in concrete material subjects, persons and dear ones like your close friends, wife etc.

The book of "Eleanor Rigby" tells the kind of marvelous story. Its main character is a young man who is born in the landlocked mountainous region of Central Asia, which during that time belonged to the completely closed USSR. After studying at a local university and becoming mentally and physically more maturate this man arrived at the conclusion and discovery that his loveliest sole mate, dearest friend of life, lived in a far away country. He eventually found her after a great efforts and searching, calculated and precisely pointed where she lives and where they could meet in the future.

http://www.amazon.fr/Telepathy-Short-Stories-Poche-Broch%C3%A9/s?ie=UTF8&page=1&rh=n%3A83649011%2Ck%3ATelepathy.%2Cp_n_binding_browse-bin%3A208613031

http://www.amazon.co.jp/s/ref=sr_pg_3?rh=k%3ALove+and+telepathy%2Cn%3A52033011&page=3&sort=popularity-rank&keywords=Love+and+telepathy&ie=UTF8&qid=1409757721

John Lennon the Great

After John Lennon, Albert Einstein, Mahatma Gandhi, Richard Dawkins, Steven Hawking and Omar Hayam there are no left other overwhelmingly religious views and conceptions except the teaching of love against war and visualization of dance in the Sun.

I thought John Lennon underestimated his own personality when he said that he did not compare himself with great prophet and that it was just accidently said in the context of great success of Beatles - we are now more popular than Jesus.

I now believed that the leader of Beatles really was greater than many others prophets who lived before him. The prophets told to us to believe them and that they would save us, as they knew the right way leading to God.

If Jesus or Mohammad had told us go and search God yourselves, sons of bitch, even if you believe to me, because I too have little knowledge about him – this would have made a much greater impression on later generations.

John Lennon said he not believe in any prophets and religions but just in love. And his generation respected and loved him for such great level of sincerity, honesty and braveness. Try to do the same thing especially if you famous and respected one that you don't believe to Allah or Jehovah. Only the ancient Kyrgyz god Tengir looks very tolerable compared with others gods and goddesses but maybe it happened due to his minority position in our society where Sunni Islam with Orthodox Russian Christianity held a leading role and just as any monopolists preferred to displace the other religions and as well as democracy.

While other prophets propagate the ideas of tolerance, patience and peacefulness and promised many a happy afterlife, John Lennon asked people with his ideas and songs to shine as stars in the current reality. He did not promise Eden somewhere in the sky but he believed that the great creativity and potential of every man and woman and society could be awakened to greatness.

He said dance with me in the sun, whenever in trouble stand with me. And what you said about such his best maxim as - create future from your images and imaginations, change and revive the stone of this senesce reality and stone of your mind. It depends on everyone, what program you feed into your mind - love or war – you will take it, what about you dream and work for in your soul and imagination that would been grown in your reality.

According to one of his key postulates, every man must shine like a star. If you believe that you are a star, no one able to disapprove you and world only want and utterly desired yours self-realization for the new superstar.

Certainly Christians and Muslims were inclined for fundamentalism find out every our comparing Lennon with the prophets as an utterly blaspheming matter. Yes, his live had not been a pristine and holy one. But what we know really about many others holy prophets? Among them had been killers, stealers, tax collectors, suppressors, makers and strikers and fighters and many others odious figures. In Islamic tradition and canon even Solomon and Alexander the Great (Iskender Zulkarnain) ranged as our ancients prophets. May I ask you - John Lennon looks very sympathetic in this long stretched scale, doesn't he?

And do not forget that John Lennon, too, was been killed as so many prominent prophets by cruel violence, shot by a rock-music fanatic and fundamentalist.

At the very least as someone who was born in the USSR I personally witnessed the greatest historical event and an absolutely incomparable and unapproachable miracle that happened in our lifetime. No other prophet could resurrect from death entire nations states the way John Lennon did, the founder of "Beatles", the greatest rock-star and prophet in our history.

Ode to John Lennon

This music has really transformed our world.
It stressed greatly the Central Asia (a previous part of the USSR) also,
in the time of Cold War and iron fences,
when our old fathers-communist leaders,
corrupted by power and the rule of the Soviet empire until death,
fighting against freedom, capitalism and the Beatles also
as well as against the decadence and poisoning art of the dying West,
until the USSR itself collapsed as a result of stupid governance
and violence and supression of the right of man.

By the way for our olders known
that according with an ancient Kyrgyz prophecy
every millennium bring to world the singer,
who might to crumble mountains and great evil empires
just with his stunning powerful songs.

Now we are going to understand
who John Lennon really was.

Thank you forever, bard of the millennium,
singer with Irish-Kyrgiz roots,
the modern Ossian,
Orpheus who saved our world
and presented freedom to the imprisoned East.
You deserved our deepest respect and love for that
from generation to generation
as long as sounds
this unusual music here and everywhere -
Mind games, Stand by me, Imagine,
Girl, Instant karma, Across the Universe.

http://www.fishpond.com.au/c/Books/q/Life+With+The+Beatles?ou
tprint=1&filter=new_releases&page=1

Удобную религию
придумали... арабы

Быть мусульманином или, по крайней мере, изображать из себя правоверного, очень выгодно, особенно если ты родился мужчиной. Кто бы не хотел иметь три и даже четыре жены, как это практикуют многие политики и религиозные лидеры и даже просто безработные на окраинах страны, которые и себя не могут толком прокормить, но, поверив наставлениям молдо, успели завести новые семьи? (С моей точки зрения, многоженство это не просто узаконенная проституция, но и разрушение генофонда нации, когда депутат ЖК обзаводится несколькими женами и плодит детей, которые будут такими же коррупционерами, как и он сам).

Кто бы не хотел, чтобы любимая женщина прислуживала как рабыня, одевалась для тебя в твоем доме, а на улицу выходила закутанная в чадру или вовсе не выходила? Еще лучше, если к такому порядку приручить женщину, которая не любит тебя и весьма строптивая нравом. Например взять в жены насильно Шарон Стоун и заставить ее подчиниться мусульманским правилам и этикету, чтобы она наряжалась только для тебя и варила манты.

И, конечно же, настоящий мужчина не заинтересован в том, чтобы женщина училась и получила хорошее образование и стала со временем даже умнее и образованнее, чем он сам. С нее достаточно, чтобы она оставалась в доме, как запертая птица и удовлетворяла ненасытные сексуальные потребности мужа. А когда она надоест тебе и состарится, можно будет легко уговорить ее, чтобы ты женился повторно. И ты, старый хрен моржовый, когда тебе стукнет 60 и даже 70, можешь взять себе в жены 16-летнюю девчонку - благо, что в слаборазвитой, полудикой и деградирующей стране всегда будут возможности, чтобы купить и любовь и жену. И если она родит тебе ребенка, еще будешь гордиться, назвав его Алтымышбеком или Жетимишбеком.

Кто будет отрицать, что это одна из самых изощренных и распространенных в мире форм сексуального рабства? У меня тоже на примете много красавиц, которых мне бы хотелось запереть в своем воображаемом гареме? Мне тоже хочется иногда, как молодым бандидам из ИЗИС, украсть семнадцатилетнюю курдеянку и преподавать ей уроки Корана в неволе? Но это тяжкое преступление, которое должно быть жестко пресекаться. Иначе мы рискуем весь мир ввергнуть в сплошное мужское насилие и произвол и передел и приватизацию всех женщин на всей планете - от 8 до 80 лет.

Но это не просто вопрос этики и морали. Как гражданин Кыргызстана я понимаю, что наша страна не выживет как самостоятельное государство, пока женская половина не будет вовлечена в процесс в полной мере, пока мы не будем опираться на образованных и сильных женщин страны, не будем их постоянно и целенаправленно поддерживать, даже если это приводит к весьма болезненным явлениям в краткосрочнои плане. Сильная и умная женщина кому-то может показаться плохим подарком судьбы, особенно если у него самого проблемы с мозгами. Но в деле выживания семьи и нации что может быть лучше, когда твоя половина не просто умеет подавать тебе оружие, но и владеет им отменно сама.

А к этому ведут только научный стиль иышления, ценности демократии и европейской цивилизации, торжество закона, образование. Только это способно спасти нашу страну и, думается, всякий истинный патриот Кыргызстана рано или поздно согласится со мной.

Into the cold: the adventure of a post-Soviet cake

Once upon a time I was a follower of the Communist religion, I sincerely believed in Marx and Lenin as all of us and our fathers had been mercilessly motivated and beaten by the instructors and commissars of the USSR. That's why all the believers from this great country have so roundly thought and looked.

But nevertheless this empire came down one happy day and all the cakes – prisoners -went out to freedom after the dismantling of the great oven. Heaven showed mercy.

But freedom and independence didn't appeal too much to the absolute majority of our freshly baked cakes. Many started again to dream about a return to the hot oven.

But I was not among them, I was fond of the newly found freedom even if I suffered severely as many others my contemporaries - freshly baked cakes if you will - from cold and hunger and frustrations during this transition.

Yes freedom sometimes looks not so comfortable as the burning oven but I moved ahead.

Between 30 to 35 years of age, I was fascinated by the traditional religion of our region and people - Islam. That also many talked about burning ovens in the afterlife for sinners and unbelievers, so it was familiar to me but attracted little and I eventually ran away from Islam as I had from Communism.

From 35 to 40, I studied the Bahai religions. Was it a very good lesson? More mild and tolerant and advanced compared with tough and odd other conception but after learning theirs study, I eventually ran away, searching something better and more in line with my convictions. From 40 to 50, I have been immersed in the study of the Bible and the teachings of christianity. I almost made a choice in favor of Jehovah's witnesses, but at the last moment before my final baptizing in the funny plastic tank in a stadium I decided to slip away for the favor of the Anglican church as the most suitable for me after such a long jorney.

But there, Western science and English and Anglo-Saxon civilization and democracy prevailed over everything and so I became an atheist or rather, I should say, an agnostic.

And now I know exactly where and how to find God: by starting to believe in, respect and love Western civilization and worship its basis, the rule of law and a pluralistic society where everyone has a place: Jews, Muslims, Christians and a great many other religions and atheists also, and where both the majority and the minority are happy, tolerant and coexist among each other, where women and children have the same rights as older men, and where the deputies and presidents ride bicycles, and the general public is predominantly opposed to the authorities who strictly control them and where there is no room for fanatism, hate and burning ovens. What could be better than that? Jonny–cake knew where to roll.

I've outlived Communism, studied Islam, Bahai, and various denominations of Christianity and I am ready to embrace Western democracy and civilization. Nothing better has ever existed and been invented, and in comparison, all others religions look like a burning oven. As a baked cake I know pretty much about such sorts of things.

http://www.lovereading.co.uk/book/9781482823578/isbn/noredirect

Если бы я был пророком...

Если бы я был пророком - не важно Иисусом Христом или Мухамедом, - то у меня среди апостолов и последователей обязательно присутствовали женщины, или даже, скорее всего, их было 50 на 50 с мужчинами. Не понимаю, какой интерес и смысл читать проповеди в компании одних мужиков? Конечно, если бы у меня среди апостолов были одни женщины и при этом одни красавицы, это было бы совсем прекрасно, но кто поверил бы такому пророку?

Но точно также недопустимо и невыносимо, когда среди последователей одни мужчины, так же как запрещать посещение мечети женщинами наравне с мужчинами.

То, как поступили пророки и их последователи, наводит на два предположения:

Либо пророки (да хранит меня мой Бог от фанатиков!) были в той или иной степени склонными к гомосексуализму, либо, как в случае с исламом, вдобавок к нетрадиционным отношениям, мужской пол не был особо заинтересован в приобщении к божественным истинам женщин.

Не хочу обвинять в гомосексуализме никого, скорее всего, все объясняется мужским эгоизмом и ревностью, когда сильный пол всегда был на первом месте и отказывал женщинам во всем - даже в общении с богом.

В результате, мы получили эту унылую и безрадостную картину, когда толпы бородатых мужиков молятся в мечети, а женщины отсутствуют.

И даже когда приходишь в гости к мусульманину, который слишком далеко зашел в своей вере, его жена не показывает своего лица, даже если это солидная дама в годах, как если бы они принимали в гости какого-нибудь сексуального маньяка.

В общем, все это очень нехорошо и мерзко, даже если это традиции, и я рад, что кыргызы никогда не были и не будут фанатами ислама, хотя будут с не меньшей страстью дорожить своими женщинами, как какой-нибудь азиат или кавказец, который готов зарезать тебя, за один лишь взгляд на его жену.

Спокойнее, товарищи мусульмане! Женщин хватит всем и скоро будет совсем хорошо, когда слабый пол наконец проснется для активной охоты на мужиков!

Jack and the beanstalk

(Kyrgyz modern version of an old English story)

Once upon a time there was a boy living with his mother in a country that severely suffered from bad kings and governors. Usually, after achieving the power they often became greedy monsters, bad boys and hideous masters of corruption. Due to quickly growing gluttony they had eaten cows, sheep, pigs, horses along with pastures where the livestock grazed, then they set about absorbing factories, farmlands, hydro-electric plants, forests, coal and gold mines, mountains, glaciers and so on. Meanwhile, the people's suffering from hunger, drought and pollution of environment were growing day by day because of them leaving nothing after such greedy, sordid and stupid management.

And it must be said, the inhabitants of country have been very responsible and actively fighting for their benefits and rights, against bad governors. At the short historical time they had overcome three folds and dismissed kings and governors of the country but we don't know why the practical results of such dismissings were no fine as citizens were waiting from revolutions. Nothing changed from these coups and overplots. Leaders and parties who came to powers after expelling demagogues and wretches, promised and swore a lot for the great future and perspectives. But then after inauguration quickly degrading and downgrading, country again severely suffered from new breed of robbers, and beggars, and thieves, and bad boys, and monsters of wild capitalism and others post-soviet parasites, filthy makers and merciless predates.

Pastures degraded, waters polluted and as a result even the cow stopped to give a milk.

And once dissipated and distressed from bad news mother said to Jack:

- Stop talking politics and watch TV, go to the market with our cow and cell it and bring home some money before we have not starved to death from such cursed reality.

Jack went to the market and, as you well informed, he got a meeting with miracle-seller who suggested him 5 bean for the old cow who stopped giving a milk.

- Take my magical bean, my boy, - said the strange-looking seller, - all nation and world look for you and wait miracles. Only miracle might save our cursed country. Please, Jack, give me your old and tough cow in exchange for these beans and you have the chance to save yourself and entirely our nation from total poverty and calamity.

OK, Jack made the good decision and returned home with the magical beans.

He planted them in the garden and after that went to sleep right on the place where placed the bean. Jack was very inventive person, he didn't want to climb up to the sky, instead he rocketed to the heaven with the quickly growing beanstalk, lying with comfort on its top leaf and slip down right to the castle where he planned to steal a golden hen and singing harp.

Yes he reached to the heaven but it looked quite differently, not as in the famous faire-tale and its multiple interpretations on TV-programmers and theatres staggering. It was the country that has floated on the aisle from cloud and called The Great Flying Constitutional Monarchy.

King of country very politely received Jack when he informed about him and his trip from the lower realm and country. Jack astonished how humble he was and led himself the highest person in the upper world. Generally kings and governors there have been very polite, modest and kind – and people, citizens and peasants contrary jealous, stubborn and impolite. King and theirs family lived without the great pretension and ambitions in the ordinary houses and the ministers and high officials going to work often on bicycles. At the same time the ordinarily people there lived in luxury and leisure, it was an excellent society, consisting from very rich and influential persons and families. They all drove very expensive cars, lived in castles, had a dinner in precious restaurants.

- How you have got such miracles? - asked boy to King.
- Because we know the secret and receipt of good governance, - proudly answered King, - called the Magna Carta and Democracy.
- What is that? - asked Jack.
- The magic sticks – told to him king, - which were prepared and designed to run harmonious states managements and services of various levels. Than higher our official are ranged, than more painfully and sharply beaten by this

sticks for the every mistakes and misconception they have done in states services

- How they do work? – asked boy.
- I give you the magical seeds – answered King, - our scientists prepared such know-how in our research institutions and labs, – and King bring to boy another portion of magical beans. - Plant them for good soil and you will see how it work.

Boy returned home and landed the magical beans. His mother was very angry when he descended without golden hen and singing harp.

- What the hell you brought another portion of the same beans from heaven!? – shouted to him mother.

But Jack relaxed her and promised really great miracle in this route.

- Look, mother, - said Jack - not only our family along will be happy and wealthy but all our unhappy country will turn to better life, long termed prosperity and safety.
- O my poor boy, - exclaimed disheartened mother. - We have nothing to eat and you babbling me about old Sugar-candy?
- About Democracy and Magna Carta, mom, - answered her well-educated and informed son
- White a little, dear, and you see all.

In the next morning from the beans grew the unusual rods with the handle and body covered with the sharp prigs. Jack never have been in Africa and have no idea about cactuses. But it is very unusual cactuses, more like to the old weapon of nomads and vikings for the beating enemies for heads, backs and buttress.

And they would moving and flying and starting to work. They are searching, hunting and beating the first rate injustices, imperfectness and cruelty that existed and flourished in the world. They beat presidents and their families and close ones, then ministers, high officials, than legislative body, than juridical system and court, than municipal governors and so on and on.

All the responsible persons in the country have been severely executed and persecuted. When rods break from heavy working or even left prigs, from every piece and prig grown a new rod, that immediately started its work.

After one week all the country had these rods in the substantial quantity for the extremely fast, diligent and efficiently works for the transformation and reformation of the all levels and grades of society and states body - for the rehabilitation and supplanting the new and responsible governance and strengthening the roots of positive changings.

Yes, these rods beat very hardly for the backs and buttress of responsible persons and officials for the every mistakes and failure. But there have been the simple antidotes against such heavy and humiliating public executions.

Major of city or deputy of parliament who have been chased by rods for the receiving bad decision under the pressure of highest body, they might for the stoppage punishment announced about resignation and execution ended after two or free final beatings

It was much worse have been for the governor involved for various bad decisions and sentences.

Rods beat them long and persistently even after their resigning until they return all stolen money and resources wholly and compensate all the losses from bad decisions. Certainly presidents, prime-ministers and leading officials who actively mixed and participated for various corruptive scandalous, executed exclusively hard, merciless and long.

After one month situation in the country changed differently with the radically way. All the governors trying panically avoid the rods worked extremely well and diligently, no one think about stealing or robbing or just for leisure and negligence, because rods beat very painfully and harmfully with their prigs.

And country very fast overfilled with the peace, happiness and welfare under the guide of magical rods of democracy and Magna Carta.

Yes it was the most beautiful faire-tale about magical transformation in our world. But it was very long time ago. Sorry that late, kings, presidents and ministers and officials again found way to escape from punishment and could reformatted and reprogrammed the magical rods with such way that they starting protect their right – not the right of justice, democracy and Magna Carta. As a result our world today again suffered from bad government and incompetence.

But people keep in soul the old recollections and songs and legends coming to us from the past times and which never dying in our memories. We end this story with a one of such old song from our heroic history called as "Graze the presidents"

Graze the presidents

Do you love people, children, country and world more than your
own life?
Than graze presidents and leaders
with heavy knots, strong sticks, iron rods.
Beat them, hart, wound their nice building carcasses,
deform their saturated with rarely ingredients bodies,
reshape their excellent trained torsos
merciless and severe
for their sake and savings and bless of nation.

All presidents and governors look as asses
able to learn and be patient
only through terrible beating and sufferings.
Only after long termed awful treatments
by own awoken people
from generation to generation
their majesties have to getting respect
very slowly and gradually
the human rights, law, justice and other firmaments
of sustained civil society,
stopping for ever
to kill the freedom and opponents,
to dream about live long presidency,
and stealing billion dollars

from the purse of country,
turning the nation
toward the Black Hole of universal corruptions.

So graze presidents, beat and teach them
if you love people and yours country
more than your safety and aimless living guarantee,
maybe well for you but so bad for your children.

http://www.ebay.com.au/sch/sis.html?_nkw=BEATLES%207%20
45%20ELEANOR%20RIGBY%20CHILE&_itemId=331190403222

http://www.amazon.fr/s/ref=sr_st_popularity-rank?keyword
s=Singapore.&qid=1409892940&rh=n%3A52042011%2Cn%
3A81604011%2Cn%3A83649011%2Ck%3ASingapore.%2C
p_n_availability%3A429338031%2Cp_n_binding_browse-
bin%3A208612031&__mk_fr_FR=%C3%85M%C3%85Z%C3%95
%C3%91&sort=popularity-rank

The brilliant from future - who stole it from us?

When John Lennon had shot in 1980, Vatslav Havel said about this tragic event as for the death of our century. Yes, we have seen on the picture of lieder of Beatles the portrait of the 20 th century. But we also could say about him as for the man from future of our World.

Anton Chekhov in the end of the 19 th century wrote, that a men from far future, who will lived after 200-300 years, would been much more harmonies, perfect and handsome. I thought Russian writer saw in his soul the image of this chap from England when cast view so far from himself but yet not so far from us who lived in the XXI century.

Look at John Lennon, read his words, hear his amazing songs and you agree with me. That is a really portrait of our century but also the one mystic capture from our brilliant future.

"If you were born, shine as the star!"

"Everyone must shine as the stars and together we able to end completely with the surrounding darkness!"

Triumph of the Dark forces?

If the John Lennon would not have shot in 1980 our world today might be a quite different than now. He had a such great energy - inexplicable and mysterious, that could completely melted and pushed down all the borders and barriers, existed everywhere and created the totally new reality. I thought no one doubted that John Lennon if he decided to participate in election he will win as the new president of USA. Maybe he had so many problem with the ordinary procedure of bringing USA citizenship for the UK citizen, because some influential people there afraid him as the next candidate for the most influential post in the world? Who were this dark forces and which the aim and goals they represented? American FIS, or Soviet KGB, or another similar structure from Islamic world, Israel? Maybe they are joined together against Lennon incredible personality?

In any case if John Lennon would been elected as president of USA it would completely transform our world, especially if we pointed the fact that this time had been extremely rich for the new possibilities. John Lennon might come to power together with Gorbachev in that time in USSR in other part of our hemisphere.

I thought they were really might not only start Perestroika but also very well ended it with the great achievements and worldwide success. As a result there were not only ended the Cold War and Berlin Concrete Wall broke down but all the barriers in the world fall down and crushed under the guide and power such persons.

USSR joined with the West and USA, the all Islamic caliphates and China and others post-communists and post-totalitarian countries also completely transformed.

Where have not been no war in Balkans, no Putin, no war in Syria, and these very costly and tragic war in Ukraine, no Custom Union of stealers and corruptive old rascals on the post-soviet space and no new Cold War between East and West, no treat of Islamic terrorism and many-many others bad challenges

All the people and countries have been tightly united and liberated and reformatted by the great genius of our modern history and culture. Who knows maybe John Lennon was a really prophet and what's more the last prophet about them so many predicted Cristian's, Judish's and Islamic's holy scriptures and mankind cold do the great leap toward the best future that we even not imagined.

Maybe John Lennon killed by the agent that sent back from the bad version of our future? Does the killer robot from Terminator- II (1990) reminds so prophetically the national lieders of great country who came in power 10 years late? Maybe Arnold's hero could not terminate him when tossed to burning liquid iron? Maybe this super robot found way for sneaking out, resurrected and repaired and later transcendenced in another side of planet where could carry out one of the most successful black overplot in modern history?

"People have the great power but they don't know about. They have not educated in sufficient level for the understanding, measuring and starting to use the immense energy belonged to him. And all we must to do - awake this power of people".

http://www.foyles.co.uk/all?term=Eleanor%20Rigby#sor=1

The secrets of great music

This music has sounded excellent and elegant. But in our world we could find plenty of songs and melodies that also very nice sounded or even extra nice.

So why and for what reason the "Beatles" had such astonishing and universal success and so many others rock bands in USSR were not?

"Veselye rebyata", "Samotsvety", "Yalla",'Dos mukasan" and many others bands from prime league of Soviet rock music also had been created by the joining efforts of very gifted, ambitious and educated musicians, they were very popular in USSR, someone from them even now very desirable in post-soviet area, but no one from these our superstars–groups couldn't compare with the "Beatles" for ounce or jotte and not produced the really great hits.

I presumed that such phenomenon extended firstly from the exceptionally fruitful soil of the super-advanced national formation like United Kingdom, England, and secondly from the such magical components as Freedom and Democracy,

Certainly I am right or very close to the truly fact. "Beatles" must be born and released only in England.

But now I thought that all explained by the prophetic person of John Lennon. The similar thing happened with the ancient Arabia where born and lived and made wonders Abraham, India who presented the world Krishna, Buddha and Gandhi, Israel where born Jesus Christy and again Arabia and Mekka where came to world another great prophet Mohammed and Russia of XIX century with the extraordinary Leo Tolstoy. Maybe need to add to that list somebody also - Shakespeare, Dante, Alexander the Great, Chingis Han? I don't know and afraid to do others steps and make new suggestions.

I just want to say John is really found the formula and mantra that capable to help people and singing about such things in the troubled times and his great success and personal tragedy maybe showed the way that would leading to save our World, everyone and all of us. Certainly we maybe could not to be as "Beatles" or John Lennon or Jesus Christy or Mark Zuckerberg but they inspired and really helped us with their extraordinarily creativity and mystical powers and we must know their way and deeply loved and respected them and trying to do what they done and reached.

The secret seems very simple.
Whatever happen in your trouble - stay with me.
even if mountain crumbled down and sky rolled up and vanished
stay with me.

I think this song give to as the best explanation and illustration the parable from Jesus Crist and Mihail Bulgakov and... also opened the core secret of Quantom theory and Big Bang about the tinniest particle of believe and love that save us and make miracles, created and recreated universes.

Do you remember the Einstenian formula? The total energy of every object equaled for it mass multiplying to the speed of light in square (multiplying to itself). It was a really big number and quantity.

Love is the vital part of our existence, it's as the speed of light, as the light itself. Nothing more might be comparing with them. Even our universe without love just a death space that will instantly collapse down and vanish forever.

All the world might be changed, our friends and dear ones left us or even betrayed but love survived and saved us. It is so simple and evidently as this great music created from great love, as the holy scripture inspired by the words and deals of Savior.

http://www.avoprime.com/search?&q=Empire&node=10303

Democracy as the most preferable kind of religion

As we said early in the one of preceding articles The Unified Field Theory for all kind religions and believers and etc. No matter for whom or what you believed, you must have own belief or selected better one among existing 2 000 religious but the most important and valuable thing for you it is have the belief and kept basic commandments well known for all believers.

Do you remember, if you have tiniest particle of belief, you will able to do miracles.

John Lennon sincerely loved and believed to Yoko Ono and we could say that his religious was been exceptionally productive. No matter how much you appreciate and love or vice-verse hate and despise Yoko Ono. Albert Einstein believed to the mystery of Universe and also gained the eternal Glory. Many people believed and loved with the same religious obsession to their close relates, parents, and even loveliest children. The traditional Buddhism and Shintoism, the religious of Chinese and Japans based on the similar sort of love and deep respect and worshiping dead forefather and old traditions. From the point of Muslims and Christians such religions looks as the blaspheming and heathenish old things and atavisms. But no one cannot now despise the great achievement of modern China and Japan. Indian people also believed for a various multiple gods as the ancient Latin's and Grecians and still saved theirs traditional religious and also might be proud with the corresponding great achievements in culture, economics and others branches. Maybe the old Latin's and Grecians also better saved their ancient empires if they would better protect and save their ancient religions from the latest invaded monotheistic fundamentalists?

But I don't want to discuss about good or bad human religious and many kinds of believes. Better have belief, the thinnest particle of it, than to try to learn others to believe when you have not it.

But if you cannot do the choice and seeking the object of belief for yourselves I warmly recommend you believe to the Democracy, starting from it.

Democracy as a religion has many privileges, better and dynamic features. It is exceptionally honest, kind, vivid and reformative by its deep nature, frame and constitution, absolutely non-dogmatic and filled with the sense and essence of reality.

What would mean for you or anybody else if you decided keep Democracy as God? How it would change your life, granted and inspire it?

I thing you blessed immediately because Democracy is the better thing in the world that have been invented or discovered for the honest ruling by people and society, for the make wise decision, for the coming to consensus, suggested methods and technologies, for the solving any sort of problems. That is kingdom of law, common sense, prudence and art for building the bests and solid structure for any kind of social self-organizations.

In the same time Democracy suggested and combined the strong competition in all part of activities for the inspiring potentially winners together with constantly sustaining the weakens parts of society, opening for both of them new ways for realization and achievements.

Democracy also means increasing sensitivity for better learning and owing all emerging innovations and better sides and features from other religious, for incessant modernization and self-motivation and unremittedly going toward perfection and success.

Yes, Democracy that is the most impressive and authentic transcendence of God. When we opened and discovered all the deepest secrets, mysteries and reviving and restoring craft of Democracy in our society and world, we also much better known about our Creator.

http://www.avoprime.com/search?&q=Empire&node=10303

Be happy in two worlds of our reality

(Extract from diary of Jolchuby, the excellent Kyrgyz jigit, who in the time of strictly guarded Iron fences bravely undermined and broken all these barriers and found out his love, lived in the other side of our planet, saved her from forlornness through extending amazing channel in dreams)

One of the mine psychological problem and very sensible superstititon of our traditional mentality still leaved unsolved that is our wrong attitudes for the some sorts of dreams, visions and thoughts also.

For example we panically don't like to penetrate into the thoughts, visions and dreams with the participations of our dead's or about them. Why? I don't know for what reason? It was naturally for children to fear various gnomes, lepricones and skeletons in dreams but why grown man and woman so afraid to meet with dear but dead mother, father and other gone relates, when they slept? And where must going after that our dead's dear?

We much more tolerable appointed in our dreams with the live people but there also have own serious and might to say awful problems.

Our spiritual and mental teachers, guides and gurus don't like when nice girls and pretty women come to us in our dreams and fantasies, our people preferred when more platonic plots emerging in our subconscious and phantasies, when we are acquainting with old wise men with long beard and turban on head. And much better would be if you have not seen any kind of vision - just sleep as dead. Any visions have got as something temptative, sinfull as something indecent.

Why and for what we so strangely received, badly motivated when have deal with such serious thing as our sleeping, the chief nourishment, one of the great journey and mystery in our life?

Let analyses this subjects eloquently and one by one.

Our superstitious fears when we have met dead in our dream explained by the our staunched religious doctrines reigned in our mentality. Islam as the some Christian religious and Judaism have strongly and often intolerable opposited to the others kind of religions, despised and humiliated the worshippers of parents, dead's, spirit's, sun, flame, forest, gardens, mountains and so on. Such superstitions have originated from heavy prejudices, as consequences of long termed often genocidal battles between the bibleistics religious and others believes and concepts existed long before of the worldwide established monopolists.

For the same reason our Islamic puritans very negatively have got any sort of dreams where we meeting with woman. All such things from shaitan told us moldo, as the protestants priest and Russian pops. We must only prayed to God and avoid any kind of fantasies and dreams. If our religious lieders have had specific equipment and modern technologies they are without doubt castrated all our dream wavers and expelled from our head any kind of fantasies and imaginative capacities.

Compare with them Tengrianism, Buddhism and Shintoism much more tolerable received such things as our healthy dreams and spiritual entertainments and others subconsciously activities, also they are more friendly, politely and delicately communicated with this or that non-ordinarily spiritual creatures, lived or trying to live in our mentality, with much more respect acquainted our dead relates - father and mother - when they coming to us in our dreams. And where also they would to go?

Some religious worshiped dead's, but tengrians didn't like and avoiding such things. They just tolerable and friendly received various kind of human attractions, believed to the spirits of dead and afterlife but they also believed for the spirits of water, heaven, Earth and other such things in theirs maltitudness.

Jolchuby, as we had seen, deeply believed to his dreams, carefully investigated and revived them and even turned them to the sort of truly sacred things - and as a result gained the great success, rewarded immeasurable, found out dear one. He was lucky because escaped as from Muslim prejudice and canons strictly prohibited such things as the flirtation with the demons and blasphemy and so he had not be trapped by communists massively long termed anti-western propaganda, comeuppances and strong psychological barriers densely planted in our subconscience by the several generations of Stalinists and Leninists.

So I wish you encountering ever with the marvelous dreams and visions and be happy and feel pretty well and comfortly whenever that happened, prepare and hone yours conscience and sub-conscience just for happiness when you seen nice girls and beautifull women or if you meet something like bitch or other strangely things and troublesome marks and signs and creatures – don't worry and prepare yourself just for happiness and nothing more - everytime and everywhere.

http://www.bokus.com/cgi-bin/product_search. cgi?ac_used=no&search_word=partridge+singapore

My grandma's fear

I remembered as my mother said to me about her mother, my grandmother, who told her once not so long before dying - please, my dear daughter, be carefully after my death with the dreams. Not think much about me and suffer especially you will going to sleep not want to meet with me in dreams. When mother asked why, grandma answered, because if I have met with you in dreams, one day I might seriously frighten and hurt you. So will be better if you not communicate with me in the dreams at all after my death, just remember me when you no sleep and do not suffer much, it would be better for both of us.

Yes, sure, my grandmother, whom I never had seen, died early when my mother was young girl, as many others Kyrgyz women and given broadly the much of eastern mothers had lived under the strong influence of Islamic and Tengrianic doctrines about our dreams and afterlife. She sincerely worried that her spirit or those who carried her spirit afterlife might be seriously wounded her dear child.

It's clearly, when we have seen dead's relates in our dream we usually expressed the fear, originated from our fears of Death.

Muslims teacher even recommend in such occasion turn out from such visions, run away and if need for that actively protect himself with praying and so on. Certainly if the vision lead itself badly and trying to retreat or even attacked you, would be better if you answered and even fight with them. It's mean that you have seen something other in you dream who just weared image of you dead relates. In any case be polite and not provoke conflict at first.

As a result of such crossroad troubles both sides - as a dear mothers and grandmothers, so their left children –seriously mentally suffered from lack of communication.

Why not to run this dreams more humanly and politely with more respect, love and courage?

If your elders want to meet with you, why we must so rude and unkind received them?

So I have strongly advised you, if you make acquaintance in dream with you dear one who departed from our world, never afraid but lead yourself politely and with good respect for Death. Would be better if you with the praying to God take your dear one with warm embrace. And I am firmly believed from such attitudes both sides filled themselves much more happy and satisfied.

If you are atheist and utterly don't believe for such things, our advice also would be helpful for you. Do you want or not but such dreams will come to you periodically and you have to with such or other way communicate with them. Why you must suffer if you see in yours dream such visions and creatures?

Look for them as for yours subconscious phenomenon and treasure or just for curious things of you mentality and past experience and work with them. They able to help if you expressed love and respect for them.

You could now just imagined, my dear friends, with how much obstacles, fears, superstitions and monsters close kept in touch our genius, good fellow Jolchuby in his long termed trip acros the sea of Dreamland before he reach and found Eleanor Rigby.

This article I want to end with my poem that I wrote 4 years ago after two month as I lost my mother. It was created on the base of my dream – one of the first meeting in dream with my mother after her death. In that time I didn't understood the cause and price of our mistakes and fatal prejudices - we just suffered separately from each other with the impermeable despairs and suffocating grieves. Who could explain the pain of mother who far gone from children not only by physical death but also by wrong and cruel misconceptions strongly prohibited any kind of deep communications and remembrances before and after?

Truth saves us in any case, false only increases our suffers

Mother's soul
(first appointment in dream)

She was weeping and suffering in my dream
without any chance for rest,
o my poor mother's soul
on the corner of crossroad
of district where I lived
so close to home and me
and so far and inaccessible
without any chance for patient and peace in her woe.
She is missing us and seeking - on the verge
quite different two worlds,
where coordinates, spaces and recollections
so devastating and wholly mixed.
I am going along her
could not to close and embrace her,
but my sister staying with her and trying to sober her
in her so deep and hopeless woe
on the verge
of crossroad of different and so hostile to each other worlds.

I am going along her
made circle around district
and again meet
this dolled pair
at the corner of crossroad.
quite near my home.
Death divided us
and forbid any chance for meeting
even in dreams.
And poor soul is weeping and suffering
without any chances for rest,
missing forever us.
as a little girl
lost in the crossroad of so odd and merciless town.

http://www.amazon.co.uk/s/ref=sr_st_relevancerank?keywords=gr
eat+love&qid=1413539858&rh=n%3A266239%2Cn%3A62%2Cn%
3A275380%2Ck%3Agreat+love%2Cp_n_binding_browse-bin%3A
492563011&sort=relevancerank

Magna Carta for nightmares

(from the diary of Jolchuby, the great traveller and investigator of our dreams)

My loveliest native land and country - Kyrgyzstan - has achieved the greatest success and breaktruth in its democratic evolutionary progress in XXII century.

While other nations and states around the imperfect world after establishing Magna Carta for human races everywhere worldwide starting to search and invent its convenient and consistent applications for others living creatures as the Magna Cartas for sheep, horses, caws and others agricultural species and then for wild beasties also, for fishes – domestic and wild, the same with insects and even some very advanced nation like Norwegians and Swedens even starting prepared Magna Carta for our very distant relates as bacteries and viruses, Kyrgyzstan overcame and show up all of them doing really great, the cosmically advanced step to future.

Our supertolerable, superpeacefull and super hospitable country firstly turn attention for the protection rights of our nightmares as for the most vulnerable and most unprotectible enigmatic creatures without any status which so long suffered from our prejudices and superstitions and cruelty attitudes and long ago belonged to the list of Endangered class of species.

The first in history of Democracy our governors and legislative bodies and lieders of HGO-sectors working together not only prepared the Declaration of rights and Constitution for nightmares but come to agreement about theirs representation in our Parliament.

As a result our Jogorky Kenesh in short time has been densely invaded and inhabited by any kind of bitches, ogres, lepricons, krugers, ghosts and so on – all these creatures found that place very comfortable and friendly for their tenant and survive.

And then Parliament produced many initiations, laws and suggestions that completely changed our lives and reality.

According with the new Constitution our legislature starting firmly demanded from our citizen submits a new Code of behaving and rules - at home, in the streets, in our dreams.

The first point of this Declaration is the demand for being very tolerable with our nightmares. If you are sleeping and meeting with them, you have not right for beating, kicking, cutting them, loudly crying and run away from them as maddening one. Your dreams legitimized as theirs space, homeland and private item and every sleeping person must be lead himself very politely there, as the civiled guest in private place of nightmares.

Also if you accidently or intentionally have met with them in your reality (sometimes happened such things) - if you crossed with nightmares on the street, at home, in office etc., you must be obliged to show the great patience and tolerance for them as for the dear friends and very desirable guests. Good relation between two worlds was strongly supported by our very progressive and reformative governments and common lieders.

As a result of such social evolutional processes and experiences our reality and dreams joined together, mutually collapsed through widely open innumerous borders and gates which thousands years separated and segregated and prevented our folks and nightmaritans from harmonies and close cooperation, deep respect, truly friendship and great love sparkling between them.

Kyrgyzstan one of the first in the world reached to the status of the country of Transcendental freedom and Liberty, where living people with the comfort coexisted and cooperated with the persons lived in past times or with their reflections, with the residents coming to us from future, with the any sorts of bitches, ghosts, lepricons and others monsters and curious persons - also widely and deeply represented - from various tradition and cultures, from past, present and future.

So Kyrgyzstan has had a such great achievement in its democratic progress that even Heaven blesses us, one day abolished the Day of Judgment and End the World for our region and population.

Yes, sure what else will able to give us the Day of Judgment, when we learned for such great peaceful and tolerable coexisting with such broad range of creatures, showed respect for the absolutely all things and potentially intentions of things desired to be originated with some or others way to something valuable in our universe?

Sleep well and be happy with the maximum comfort, safety and progress toward the best future, dear Mankind!

http://www.barnesandnoble.com/s/Great-love?csrfToken=ehgu5kU 9gdWmEJQgT4WV5DhERvZ4CxRR&sort=R&size=30&aref=151 9&csrftoken=ehgu5kU9gdWmEJQgT4WV5DhERvZ4CxRR&dref =1%2C9%2C145&keyword=Great+love

The tengrian praying at sunrise

For the 80 million Kyrgyz's people
who had lived ever before
since the beginning of life,
and for the 5 millions who are living now in our land,
for the immense number of others our relates
who is proceeding to live giving the birth for many great nations
and countries
in Asia, Europe, America and others continents,
who had been happily dispersed or severely and cruelly assimilated
by others culture and identities.
in any case your offspring's have been widely distributed and
dispersed and not vanished at all,
they are all bearing the ancient Kyrgyz immortal's genes of their
great forefathers,
who once upon a times in the past millenniums ruled by most part
of this world
and had been very prosperous, influential, smart and inventive.

So I turn for all you - living and lived in our planet,
as for my close relates, forefathers, cousins who survived and lived
in glory, pride and victory
or declining in progressively depressed states
in various corners of this Globe,

I turn to all of you
arise, activate and come to help us
as for your children that now so hardly survived
in small part left from our great empire,
please help to save Kyrgyzstan,
protect its independence.

We know that most part of the world
originated from our great forefathers,
many of them announced now
as our enemies,

please, open their eyes
let our ancient powerful and strong relates
and their offspring's
awake and coming to help us
and stop war, open and secret, and genocidal long term pressure
against our country and freedom,
have lead for systematically diminishing and weakening
our small nation
and downgrade mentality and state,
who was been the greatest
and most influential
in past centuries.

Let our sons among the lieders of China.
Israel and Arabia
Russia, US, West Europe, Japan, India, Brazil and Australia
coming to help us and our freedom and independence,
let most successful and richest persons worldwide
starting to invest to our freedom/ educations and independence

not for our enslavery, stupidity, self humiliation,
going for new colonization
through massively bribe our lieders and flourishing corruption.

O great Tengir, who lives everywhere and forever,
arise, revolt the eternal greatness and immortal power of
Tengir-Too.

http://www.amazon.cn/s/ref=nb_sb_noss_1?_mk_zh_CN=%E4%
BA%9A%E9%A9%AC%E9%80%8A%E7%BD%91%E7%AB%99
&url=search-alias%3Dstripbooks&field-keywords=partridge%20si
ngapore&sprefix=partr%2Cstripbooks

Magna Carta for animals

All animals, birds, fishes
and others species
which you hunted, shot, cut, killed and ate in your life's span
coming to you soon after death
in yours personally Judging day and resurrection.
Think strongly about that, friends, uncles, relates and jeneshki,
when prepare finishing next beef, ham, burger, shashlyk, hargis,
kasy-karta,
animals also in new world know own right, democracy and Magna
Carta.
Hundreds sheep, thousands hens, turkeys, dozens cows, horses and
camels and oxen's
tightly surrounded you and severely asked
why you had been so cruel with yourself evolutions brothers and
sisters?
You could not run away from their horns, teeth, beaks and heels.
If you escape from them and climb up to mountain,
dears, gouts, elks, rabbits and partridges
which killed by you in past time, attacked and toppled down you
merciless,
if you slip away to rivers and lakes or even hide in seas and oceans,
you would chastised by thousands trout's, tunas, crabs, squids,
lobsters and turtles'

that you gourmandized at clubs, restorants, otels, presentations and parties.

It's absolutely truth – the souls of every living creature that you have or have not yet are immortal.

What would you do, how save life from such looming troubles?

So be wise, while you live and have room for maneuver and reforming

try to stop hunt and kill animals, birds and fishes,

instead starting protect their lives

and recover their environment,

save wild and domestic creatures

and maybe those whom you saved

save and protect you in new world

when you will be hunted by animals killed and eaten.

How many lives kill and ate you?

How many lives protect and save you?

Keep firmly this account and balance

if you want survive in the last battle

when you soul so steep to another world to shuttle.

http://www.amazon.com/s/ref=sr_pg_2?rh=n%3A283155%2Cn%3A17%2Cn%3A10300%2Cn%3A10307%2Ck%3Agreat+love&page=2&sort=relevancerank&keywords=great+love&ie=UTF8&qid=1413649673

http://www.shop.com/search/Fragile+Empire+How+Russia+Fell+In+and+Out+of+Love+with+Vladimir+Putin+Hardcover+?k=30&sort_popular=&t=0

The tengrians praying for evolution

The total number of people who had lived in the Earth from the beginning reached 150 billion, 20 times more than living now 7 billion. For everyone living we have correspondingly 20 dead's.

So if you turned to all of them when you make early morning praying and search supports, advices and helps from the past, passed lives as for yours dear ones from the very beginning of times, if you mentioned and respect all of them, your namaz would be rewarded with multiple ways.

Just imagine 150 billion your predecessors from various epochs and cultures and continents - your potential and really ancestors and donors of you genes, if you sincerely expressed gratitude for the such vast number of souls, you would be rewarded immeasurable, joining and absorbing by the great ocean of conscience and sub-conscience of our world and human civilization.

Think about it!

What if you added to them the souls of others creatures, living now and ever had lived in our planet? Domestic and wild animals, birds, fished, reptiles, snakes, insects. Human species only one unit from millions other creatures and youngest among them, where even simple organisms have had extremely highest information contents.

Add to them the much more outnumbered animals, who lived from the beginning of our evolution, the souls of extinction species, that had lived millions and 100 million years before man, before mammals, before birds, reptiles, fishes - pray for all them who belonged to the 95% of all extinct species but many of them reigned in past dozens and 100 million years compare with much more short history of mankind's arise.

We don't know nothing about future and how would be successful human in the scale of surviving rate compare with others animals. There are existed lot of evidences and predicts that time for surviving for mankind might be the shortest among all others animals. Man has lived in Earth no more than one million years. Such modern creatures as cats, wolves, monkeys 10fold older. Crocodile originated and kept the same shape and body 100 million years. Same with sharks, our favorite sturgeons and belugas, and such species as squids and octopuses existed unchangeable more than 400 million years with the highest improved nerve system and brain.

We said that 95% of all species in our World now extinct. Yes sure, but they lived and survived very long time compare with our life span that so fast declined now.

But they are all lived in our genes.

Pray for them, search support from them, asked them to help you to survive and gain success.

This world have teamed with various forms of life and transcendences. Ask energy and help from them, because all of us that living now and had lived once in our past are immortal creatures. No one species and their represents died and vanished at all. Not only human beings but absolutely all living creatures – from our loved dogs, cats, sheep, caws to the linux, eagles, falcons, from extinction mammals and birds (from our activities and bad management) to the dinosaurs, pterosaurs died with natural ways – all of them proceed their existing and life or changed for others form of life. And all of them presented in our genes as the multiple conserved intentions of living forms.

And that also no end of our calculations. According with last revelations of genetics for everyone of living creature had born and grown were existed the great number our not born close relates, that never rise up from primarily state. Absolutely everyone in Earth have had brothers and sisters outnumbered of grains dust of Sahara desert – 30 million trillions units. Multiplicate this great number for all the people who lived in our planet from the beginning and you would appreciate the potential of our life, his richnes, because all this creatures had own mark and uniqueness. The same calculos with absolutely all others living creatures who living or had lived in our planet clearly depicted you the greatness of enigma of life.

Pray for all them, for yours close and distant relates, for your close and distant outnumbered majorities, asking help and support from that greatness, because all these souls existing and living as the primarily intentions of our universe searching innumerous ways for transcendences.

Be happy and lucky forever – flaying and reviving above the majority and inspired and revived the vast majority and be revived, inspired and supported by them!

http://www.amazon.in/s/ref=nb_sb_noss_1?url=search-alias%3Dstripbooks&field-keywords=partridge%20singapore&spr efix=partr%2Cstripbooks
Свернуть . Перевести

Dream and Reality

Reality cheats his sister dream:
why people thought about your so mystically?
you lived ever when they slept
what the misery choice and existence!
you just my fragile shadow, blurred reflection
on something mirror like very unclear and distantly,
why poets so intrigued by you, sister?

And dream answered to reality:
look, you observed only small fraction of world
and you view very facial, frigid and frozen stone-like
though filled with sun light and colorful and blissful.
But my realm and vision
much more deeper, broader and contented and complex
than what you have imagined and counted as Reality.

http://www.amazon.cn/s/ref=sr_pg_1?rh=n:658390051,k:partr
idge+singapore&keywords=partridge+singapore&ie=UTF8&
qid=1408587552

The tengrian praying at sunset

For the all living creatures
who wandering, flying or crawling in Earth
or swimming in our oceans, seas, lakes, and rivers
prosperous now or close to extinction,
for the all 95% of all species
that had lived early in past
but later totally extinct,
for the souls of billions and billions
our various predecessors
who lived once and who not lived at all
but whose quantity and potentions outnumbered massively
any our achievements but who never was born
had not such luck as those who lived or living now
and sending genes for future.
I turn for all of us who born and unborn,
bound or unbound for progression of life
but whose names and unique codes had equally fixed in Book of
Eternity.
I pray for all of us
and asking your support, advises and energies
because I have sincerely believed
that your lives and intentions to be alive had not been aimless and
vain,
and you are shell be rewarded in future

we are all, brothers and sisters,
close relates and cuisines
in our oldest planet
under this great Sun
in the pulsating endlessly universe
from Big Ban to Big Collapse
and again and again
expressing and preparing
innumerous lives form and existences.
You said there not any gods and room for them,
but who played with Quantum physics this game?
Hell with all of them,
because I sincerely believed
that our massively sufferings
inevitable changed for massively happiness
and resurrection,
when all existing and preexisting intentions and tendencies
happy or not so or destroyed mercilessly in seeds
once have find and never lost their flourishing and peacefully
transcendences.

http://www.chapters.indigo.ca/home/search/?keywords=Eleanor&la
ngtype=4105&facetIds=528239|

Missing part of the Beatles

My book in the top–list among the 300 various items (musical, historical, fiction) about "The Beatles".

O yes, I have dreamed about it very long, I was clearly and precisely remember when I firstly heard the music that stressed me instantly and deeply. It had happened in august evening at the edge of our marvelous Issyk-Kul lake in 1972 where I rested with my mother, old and little brothers at the Cholpon-Ata resort.

After evening meal in café of sanatorium (called pansionat) I walking along the two flour cottages, and suddenly I heard the unusually beautiful music, that sounded at the distance from the dancing sport where played the local band group. It was, as I will know late, the interpretations of "Girls". Certainly I went toward the dancing spot and stayed close to the band group together with several young boys also very inspired by the musical skills looking carefully for the every movement of musicians, especially for the art of solo guitarist – the blonde Russian young man - who was been really good master of his business. They are not singing, just playing the music's of popular Western rock bands and young men and girls dancing on the sport and we boys and musical fans leaning on metal parapets looking for the musicians on the edge of beautiful Kyrgyz sea.

They played the music's of many best bands and authors but I loved deeply the "Girls". It was really the love from first hearing.

I repeated in my memory this melody trying to fixed it. But the next day I cannot remember it. I have not any musical education for scribe it with notes. But I never forgot about divine music.

Eventually, after two or three months in the dream I remembered this mizic and from that time never forgot it, repeating and singing as often as possible.

In the next summer my brother Kalyinur – the student of Bishkek technical university – in the vacation days brought to our home in the south of Kyrgyzstan the several cassettes for sound recorder (magnitophone) and pictures of pop art artists, and I firstly in my life heard the original sound of "Girls" and John Lennon's voice and had seen the image of the nice man who late after his tragical death called by the other great man and refomator in politic Vatslav Havel as the portrait, image and inspiration of our century.

http://www.fishpond.com.au/c/Books/q/Eleanor+Rigby?rid=1241065199

Expanded model of universe of new and old born books

My book "Eleanor Rigby" (hard back edition) has occupied 12 place among the 3,5 thousands others hardbacks items on the Australian bookselling site "Fishpond.au" at a category for "bestsellers."

It's very good result for me, because all of that books had been published at last 10 years by various worldwide companies and selected for that panel by experts of Fishponds as valuable and relevance readings. You must assessed a selective rating of this company from the next simple fact – from 450 books published this year by Partridge Singapore only 4 items had been received by Fishponds.

That is really a company who made deal with the stars or with the books which pretended and show strong pertinence to be a star, to find with such or other ways as short, explosive so long termed interests for worldwide readers

So my book shining as a newborn star among the great number of others and belonged to the first class of stars from prime division.

Predominant part of others newborn books that published as mine in this 2014 year took places on positions between 900 and 1300, close to the middle part of list.

In the last part of list we have seen a books published 8-10 years ago, even more older. They also belongs to the stars and bestsellers but they very well distributed around the world and had familiar as the classics.

So books like the stars in our expanding universe. We have seen old stars on the great distance and more young that more close to us and many new born stars which brightly shining around and just starting their widely distributing and expanding.

Yes, this processes reminded expanding, accelerating model of our universe from several point of views.

Firstly, the quantity of publishing books in the world grows with the exponential law. Nowadays just for one month published more new books than 50 years ago for one year. In the last year in US issued 300 thousands new books and 150 thousands in UK and nearly 4 thousands in Kyrgyzstan.

For comparing bring the several facts. Today little Kyrgyzstan issued more books than Russian empire in the beginning of last century. All survived writing artifacts that had reached to us from the ancient Egypt and Sumer, 4-2 millennium before our doors might be prepared and shaped to one middle size and volume book. Same with the ancient Judaic scriptures, that united to Holy book and kept and survived in that format.

So the book printing and publishing prosesses accelerated and expanded as our uneverce as our knowledge about the world where we living.

Secondly, never we have not such easily and broad access to this immensely growing treasures. Never in past times we could look so deep to the far corners of our universe and carefully investigate them. Thanks for Hubble telescope in Earthly orbit and modern printing technologies, e-books, kind-books, Internet and so on.

Thirdly, in spite of great expanding and accelerating technologies and knowledge's, we are still very little informed about cosmos outside and inside us, we just starting learning and do first steps for creating the new schools and system of education and self-education.

How much discoveries waiting for us, how much books must been write! We just at the beginning of new great advance and leap to future! Universe and art of publishing are just accelerating forever! O dear reader or dark matter!

http://www.become.co.uk/partridge-publishing-singapore-1511-kisah-sebuah-kota-ebook--compare-prices--sc623592317

http://www.eurobuch.com/buch/isbn/9781482823578.html

The touch of genius

I've sometime asked myself what matters most in making a brilliant achievement when I remembered about our champion and one of our sports legend Shamil Abbyasov. Personally for me this name means much more than for others our citizens - for the simple reason - I had met him early than others, having chance looking to him in his child's and teenagers years.

It happened at spring of 1968 year in Osh during the towns competitions among schools. He studied in famous general school located in west side of town, named by the Russian abbreviation "VLKSM" in the honor of Soviet Youth Organization. I was graduated in equally famous school, located in central part of Osh and named for the honor of Russian scientist M. Lomonosov.

We were both eleven years children, studied in 4th form but in different schools and lived in different districts of Osh.

He and his master, extravagantly looking woman, turned my opinion among the dozens and even hundreds children collecting for sport competition in the central stadium. From the first instance I understood that this boy have been favorite of town's Olympiad. And I didn't mistake. His image and image of his teacher fixed in my memory late when Shamil won the championship in the run for short distance (60 meters) among the fastest boys of Osh.

It was a really big step ahead if you pointed the fact that Osh a town with the more than 20 secondary schools in that time, and it was a really miraculous event to overrun for the short distance so great number of young competitors.

Yes, Shama was a really miracle and beyond any competitions and comparisons in that years.

Free years later when we studied at 7 forms for the short and maybe happiest time in my life I had chance for much close observing the establishing of early stage of great sportsman. We trained together in the green field of the same Osh stadium with the group of young athletes nearly 20 boys and girls, having selected and joined from various schools of Osh for exercising 3 time per week under the guide of famous trainer Vladimir Zvyagintsev. Technically it was a best team of young athletes – sprinters, stayers and jumpers of Osh town.

In course of this exercises I knew him better, looking how he communicated with a friends, how training, running, did his jump - long and triple. Generally he was vivid and sensitive boy who did his practice with joys and jokes and various tricks. In that time he was famous as the fastest sprinters among teenagers of south part of republics where lived nearly 1,5 million people in that time. Many known about him in our local sports circle that this boy the best sprinter among the our children, some believed that he might had the good luck in republic level, maybe, if he will work hard but no one else including him, his parents and trainer don't know that he was potentially the best athlete in our world.

What he has done, how starting exercise, run, sprinted, sprang to long jump or to his favorite triple jump - that always have a great impression to me and others teenagers who trained with them. He was born with amazing and flawless technic. He looks among the children as a pearl and he was a really pearl as one of the most talented boy of our reality.

Its pity that I trained with them only three months from 15 August to early October 1971 when studying in general schools and sports exercising also of south region of Kyrgyzstan stopped for cotton picking company that usually lasted one month. And close to the end of year my family made to departure from Osh to the Nookat district according with my father's new appointment as the head of local Communist party committee and I never more meeting with Shamil Abyassov.

Theoretically I had chance to close communicate with him in 1976-1981 years when we graduated at the same institution - Politechical University of Bishkek, we even lived short time in one dormitory right in the crossroad of Achunbaev and Manasa streets. But I never have been on friendly term with him and addition to it was a days and years of his intensively growing and intensively physical exercising - so even his close relates and friends could not meet with them as often as they want - when he will won step by step republic, regional sports competitions and USSR championship and eventually the European championship in Grenoble.

Extract from

WORLD HERITAGE ENCYCLOPEDIA

Shamil Abbyasov (born 16 April 1957) is a retired athlete, who represented the USSR and later Kyrgyzstan. He specialized in the long jump and triple jump.

Abbyasov won a bronze and a gold medal at the 1981 European Indoor Championships in Grenoble. His gold medal was in triple jump with an indoor world record of 17.30, that lasted for three weeks.

Abbyasov is married to Tatyana Kolpakova and has three children. He has a degree in mechanical engineering and has worked in the field after retiring from sports.

Extract from handbook for practice English dialogues

- I've sometime asked myself what matters most in making a brilliant achievement?
- To my mind a natural talent is the thing
- I don't think so. Talent along will not get you anywhere.
- Well, it goes without saying that one must have a good lack as well.

But strong will, personal intention and good environment are of utmost importance, I believe.

http://www.kalahari.com/s?N=4294966903+11296&No=0&Ntk=def&Ntt=Eleanor&Ntx=mode%2BMatchAllAny&searchCategories=4294966903+11007

Glory for science and critical thinking

I am very proud and grateful
for such our prominent contemporaries
as Charles Dawkins, Loran Crouse, Sam Harris,
Christopher Hitchens, Carl Sagan, Steve Hawkins
and many others persons brilliant and rarely meeting
among the innumerous towns and states in the world.
Thank you very much
for helping me escaped at all
from various prejudices, locks and traps
so divisively invented and so densely have set
in our spirits, thoughts, societies,
that diminished our courage,
wiped out our holistic and energy
and our vitality and power decomposed.

I am feeling now much better
after graduating in yours universities,
than whenever else
in my past life and experiences
when I driven by the Communist party
or with the religious of my forefathers
or by a modern various ideologies and tendencies.
Glory for science and critical thinking,
all others things from Rumpelstitskin.

http://www.amazon.com/s/ref=nb_sb_noss_1?url=search-alias%3Dstripbooks&field-keywords=partridge%20singapore&sprefix=partridge+singapore%2Cstripbooks

The great magic of love

My book has surrounded by the excellent scientific and magic works that so harmoniously and friendly supported and enriched its ideas, values and content.

Duel with the Darkness, (2012),

Fatal Strategies (Semiotext(e) Foreign Agents), (2008),

The final countdown: What Isaac Newton failed to discover, (2014),

And "Eleanor Rigby"(2014), the story about building telepathic bridge between two continent.

The Kyrgyz young man who was born in remotest mountain village in Central Asia and English girl from the Darltown at the North-East of Britain subconsciously had loved each other from the beginning. They were sought each other firstly in the fantasies, then in the rarest dawn dreams, then in telepathic dreams and visions.

Eventually they were after many troubles, tests, calculations and inspirations to find each other's in dream, come to agreement about appointment - meeting in reality. The date of acquainting accounted and precisely pointed by the genius of truly love. And two lovers that all life had sought each other, found the magic keys of access to love in reality. It was happened 1980. Eleanor Rigby arrived to Moscow and exactly in time came to the Read Square right to the point under the monument of Russian historical heroes.

http://www.amazon.de/s/ref=sr_pg_2?rh=k%3AProphet+or+Clairv oyant%3F%2Cn%3A52044011&page=2&sort=popularity-rank&ke ywords=Prophet+or+Clairvoyant%3F&ie=UTF8&qid=1408288630

Nostradamus

(from the talks on the slope of hill)

- Well, do you know, chap, I have now my own pretension for this great prophet Nostradamus, while he was a really good fellow, wasn't he?
- What you said? Nostramus? Mean a bird from Africa? Or... this bird called... stramus... yes... strays. Yes, it is a big bird with completely naked legs, running very fast, eh... But maybe I am mistake again? OK. I am remembered. It was not a bird at all. It was a great flying dinosaur called Orniticarus, am I right?
- What the hell you bubling, Kozuby baike? I am telling you about Nostradamus! (pointed finger to the blue heaven). Do you undestand me! Nostradamus. How badly to teach in University where you studied if you after all don't know about Nostradamus?
- Absatar baike, don't forget that I studied long ago, and addition to after university worked only 5 years in branch and returned again to our village and from that time grazing the sheep and gouts on this hills. So I forgot many sciences −zoology, biology. But interesting that I am remember still the dinosaurs and diplodocus that we are learned in additional curses for keeping whole level of education. Forgot veterinary science and what we did in

lab but still remember the bone features of giant jaws of pliosaurus and eating hobbits of seismozaurs.

- Wel, well, it looks as if you did learn and prepare in your universe for grazing dinosaurs, not for sheep, didn't' it?

- Not joke about my education. And what is the chap was been your Nostramus?

- I said you Nostradamus not Nostramus! He was a greatest prophet who lived in sixteen century in some small town in France and, only imagine, in his dream or when he was deadly drank he saw all happened in future. Himself stayed in sixteen century but look what happened late everywhere on Earth, long late.

- What the hell you say? How it was been and what he saw?

- He saw Hitler, Stalin, Lenin and other great persons, several presidents of USA, Paster and other prominents, who lived late many years ago after death of Nostradamus. And how he had seen! It was seems as if he sat with them around the table freely discussed and drank with them. Nostradamus pictured in his book the moustache of Stalin, the dress weared him, which the habits had and gave many others stunning features, observations and conclusion, what sometime didn't understand what they mean. What is the great person had been this Nostradamus! He was completely other compare with our up-to-day astrologists, prophets, white and black magicians, - let them all catch by hell —they are all talking lot of things but nothing wise and certain. I said you, Kozuby, if you want to be a prophet – be as Nostradamus or go out to hell. They are all done mad us, we have seen them on TV, read their prognosis in newspapers, heard by radio. All of them told, tell and will tell about coming end of world, presses our mind with such horrors and as you see, this hellish end prolonged again and again and all our waiting and preparedness go to hell.

I say you, if you want to be a prophet be as Nostradamus.

- And what he said, your Nostradamus, about the end of World?
- Hm...How to say... He, seems, also escaped to tell about such things straightly but also many feared us with the various sad and gloom things looming from the future and perspectives. It seems future ever bring us and drift us more and more toward bad things and completely forgot about goods.
- What you say with them?
- According with Nostradamus, in a future for us prepared only wrong things. Than more we are going to future, than more various monsters and confirmed person meeting us, then more stresses, calamities, droughts, wars and woes waiting for us. Saying simple for us in a future will prepare only hellish things and the happiest old days and communism were over long ago and never return again. Do you undestand me?
- And what your prophet said about our Communism epoch?
- Very good. It utterly interesting question. How explain you, Kozuby, this Nostradamus talking lot about USSR but had seen from his sixteen century only bad sides of our soviet living and existing and in the same time avoiding or didn't observe the good thing that were belong to our great USSR and shared with all of us. How to say, he many told about how died our people, the enemies of soviet rule and Red Army, how they worked and frozen in camps and

lagers near Norilsk, Magadan and other parts of Siberian, how fired up thousands people without any judgment and investigation, how froze to stone deported nations – all such cruel things written in his verses, you even don't sleep after such reading.

But Nostradamus wrote nothing about our happy living. About how we were living happy and happy worked under the guiding our comrades on collective farms, how reached records of socialist workings, how much milks produced our farmers and dairies, how much hays moved and collected our collective farms, how well we were living all, how rested, relaxed and drunk a vodka - nothing about them mention in his surveillance for long future.

While we could understand him, because he was the real prophet and saw better from his far away site. He saw our world as one whole object and put together various centuries, epochs, kingdoms and regimes and certainly better knew what happened with us and around and what was better and worse.

By the way, in last year's more and more people and historics said, that soviet regime were been deep related with fascist regime in Germany. Here and there, they said, were killed millions of completely innocent people. So even if we are sometimes feeling nostalgia for soviet times and even now many of our citizens from old generation lasts believe more for Stalin and Lenin than to a God, nevertheless I count Nostradamus had been right and sow for roots of thing happened around and precise separated bad things from good.

-   Maybe it was happened according with belonging him to ruled class of France and certainly your Nostradamus, as enemy of poors, hated our colhoses and sovhoses? Our

Stalin for instance announced immediately him as a cursed enemy of people and fastly sent him to Siberia or even repressed him?

- Yes, certainly! He would done in. But his hands were short to do it. In the same time Nostradamus was able to reach Stalin from his sixteen century, jerked him for his famous and horror mustaches, looked secretly not only how that governor killed millions for statistics, but also how he had extracted in his trousers in one of the first days of Second World War.

- You are kidding!

- Not at all! I swear, I read about it. It s going to be a clear now that Stalin, you don't believe Kozuby, was not only cruel and callous man but when the deal touched personally him and his safety, healthiness and comforts he was absolutely shameless. You don't believe but he was put on in trousers in his room in Kremlin if he badly want to do it and don't want spent time for go to closet and keep decency. He hated such things when questions touched the government interests.

Once he took a crap right in the magisterial way, when moving in car with lot of other cars.

Honestly say the top governor and leader of nations must not to risk for trifles but why not to go a backside for the bushes with bodyguards and made there your deals with more comfort and pleasant?

But what likes me in Nostradamus much at all that is as he painted in his verses the world wars.

A plane is flying in sky he called as "iron bird", submarine swimming in bottom of sea as a great "iron fish" who attacked and drown war ships swimming in surface.

The underground in London he called as "ways digged under the city" and also gave picturesque about moving trains as chained with each other carts with people sitting on them. Not forget that in time when lived Nostradamus, the world knew nothing about underground, plane, jets, cars and other latest inventions and Nostradamus saw all of them in his dreams.

By the way a helicopter described him as a giant iron beetle with people sitting inside it and looking around trough little round vindows on the bark of beetle and screw named him as two big knives above the top point of beetle's back.

-   It is astonishing! And where you read about such wonders?
-   In the book written by Nostradamus, called "Sentures" with commentaries from modern scientists.

Ten days ago my niece came from Bishkek and presented this book for me.

America in that times was only discovered, but Nostradamus described New York as the great city, contained "the steep mountain like buildings". And gave us the precise coordinates of Hew York, while it absolutelydon't exist in that time. Isn'it a truly marwell?

Also Nostradamus expressed the deep respect for our... muslim peoples. He said that in close future for us great Muslim leader come to the world whom united all believers and will go to war against Christians and even will gained victory upon them, possessed the much part of world.

By the way our Muslim leaders also sometimes said about such perspectives, they are don't know about Nostradamus and not read his book, but they said that Koran contented similar prognosis.

- Its mean that in a future we will rule by the world?
- Yes, Nostradamus said about it but not for long time and honestly say such future don't attract me.
- Why? Doesn't it excellent if we are all one day start to rule by world?
- How to say. It's sound attractively but think about 20 or even 30 years of wars with Europe, America, Russian, China. What's the hell will been transform our world? Better avoid with some or other way such calamities. Honestly say for me, Kozuby, the happiest time in the history was the epoch of Brejnev but before the Soviet invasion to Afghanistan. I am counted that this war was one of the top mistakes of our government. If we didn't starting this war maybe USSR didn't destroying.

But we talked lot of damn things to day, Kozuby baike, about this steep prophet Nostradamus. He knew all and all prepositioned and shoved.

But I had one pretension for this Nostradamus. If he was so wise and sow everything what happened in a future and how who thought and how gone to closet or lay down right to asphalt or if some unknown killer hidden in bushes and fired a president mowing with escort, why on earth he didn't mention me in his "Sentures?"

- You mean you… Absatar?
- Yes, me!

- You are joking? Who are you for would been observed by Nostradamus?
- Not smile, Kozuby! I am the rightful man in the world, never done wrong things.

I don't believe that Nostradamus not seen me as I was sitting here in this green grass and open hills almost 20 years and graze the sheep. Yes, I know that I am not a great person but from the other side if he mentioned me in his verses it was only made more respect to him. It would been great if he wrote about me so and so in the first part of 21 century in the Rahmanjan villages lived man named Absatar, shepherd with round face. Who have moustache, sit down here in the nearest green hills from early morning till the evening, that he never done wrong things for anybody. That was sound good if he wrote something like about me, wasn't that?

And by the way I am the father of nine children and very respected shepherd. How it was happen that Nostradamus didn't observed me? Ay, I don't believe for that. He sow me I know it perfectly but I was ignored by him.

He was obsessed, over inclined with the describing Stalin, Hitler, Napoleon, kings of Europe, for various wars, conflicts, massacres and slaughters and others wrong things. It was wrong historical position and attitude itself and great mistake and unforgiving unjudgment when the world concentrated his visions only for various evils, maniacs, wicked ones, bloodsuckers and not seen the honest and right ones.

I am respecting and completely consenting with Nostradamus
but why on earth he didn't mention me, Absatarus?
Yes, Nostradamus was right and astonished

he had predicted Stalin, Lenin, Hitler
and others evil creatures
that glorified in time
but lately shamed and vanished.
He showed clearly these leaders
from farest... XYI centures
as they repressed people,
killed millions in concentration lagers
and in World Wars I and II
prepared and burned cowardly by themselves.
He also depicted very carefully
as king of France was beheaded,
as Paster invented vaccine,
and Napoleon army
invaded Europe,
and he had seen
who really killed the president of USA
the hidden sniper from bush,
and when our world come to end -
God bless us, we have several centuries in reserves.
He was right, honest and excellent
but I am astonishing personally -
how could he not mention me
the simple and honest Kyrgyz shepherd Absatarus
who practically all his life grazed sheep
on the green, open and waste pastures of Birke.
I were practically all my days
lying down on green grass
and Nostradamus just could not captured my fat body
If he really look for future through XVI century.
Inasmuch as I never been as Stalin,

Lenin, Hitler and others monsters,
no killed and destroyed anybody and nothing
and additionally have been good parent
as father of 9 grown excellent children.

Through the dreams to reality

The Kyrgyz young man who was born in remotest mountain village in Central Asia and English girl from the Darltown (Darlington) at the North-East of Britain subconsciously had loved each other from the beginning. They were sought each other firstly in the fantasies, then in the rarest dawn dreams, then in telepathic dreams and visions.

Eventually they were after many troubles, tests, calculations and inspirations to find each other's in dream, come to agreement about appointment - meeting in reality. The date of acquainting accounted and precisely pointed by the genius of truly love. And two lovers that all life had sought each other, found the magic keys of access to love in reality. It was happened 1980. Eleanor Rigby arrived to Moscow and exactly in time came to the Read Square right to the point under the monument of Russian historical heroes.

The hit of master

It's really hit of greatest Master,
when millions others run as a dreamwaster...
Could you find in dream
where deployed the largest empire
and then a town in its area
and a street in the town
and a home and a window
of the room where grown and wait you

your love
so carefully hidden by times and distances
yours dearest one - yours love indispensable
the perfect one created for you and one else.
This hero did it – find the love and save her
from sharp talons of forlornness.

I could not to do that
to find and save my personal love
that would wait me all her life in vain
somewhere, maybe, in south latitudes...
As a million other persons around the world
no prepare for great honor and attribute
I cannot find, calculate and win my real passion.
But Jolchuby did it,
he found his authentic girl - not as we were all
the millions romeos of loss and wastes
so he is really great hero in history
who able explain, resolve and win the loves mystery.

http://www.foyles.co.uk/witem/fiction-poetry/
eleanor-rigby-the-chronicles-of-great-love-and-fall-of-

How catch the dream

For the reaching to Eleanor Rigby in his dream Jolchuby had done what usually did the champions in science, sports, poetry and various others branches and entertains.

He worked on the limits of his power burning himself and his carrier, submerged in the world of irretrievable discoveries and did it for the love receiving it as the greatest prize. Usually in the sports and science and all others brunches the most talented and motivated for success persons have reached to the victory. That's why Jolchuby find his love and great obstacles and barriers did not stop him because he really valued his dreams and believed them and carefully prepared himself for the final run and championship and eventually caught his dream when others not show the such level of diligence or spent all powers and gifts for the reaching others sorts of values – richness, achievement in carriers, science and others aims.

In the instants of great acceleration of mind and spiritual activity something happened not only in our soul, in our inward world but onward, outside reality also reacted for our activities. Our time, dimensions, space, stoned reality going to change his hard staff transformed for more plactic substances answering for such phenomena. That's why Jolchuby have the access to the Eleanor Rigby and the same time changed the word thank for his great love.

It was as the telepathic phenomena, that happened and changed our environment instantly. The strongest impetus of love breaks all distance and obstacles. Sorry that 99,9 percentage of people not understand or underestimate of power of love or come to right conclusion too late.

The bandwidth signal

The secret signal
has hit our heart
as a sharp sword.

The secret signal
has obliged
for first rate transmission right,

As an emergency car
flying on the busy streets
breaking the all rules
with switched sound,

As an urgent telegram
crying about death of close one
when you received only solemn and cut words
about tragic lost and wouldn't able to do nothing more.

O yes,
there are has the deep telepathy
and the hidden channel
between all livings creatures in the world,
accecible and understandable
without any words
in the tragic instants of our existence.

So in the eve of great disaster or
catastrophe
something unusually happen
in the core of substamses and universe around us.
Men, animals, birds, reptiles
trying survive personally
starting to think and do collectively
have transformed behaviorally as close brothers,
when even cruel predators and theirs preys
run out from flames skin to skin
under strong demand of that bandwidth signal.

And so in the end of Times,
as clearly witnessed holly scriptures
not only all living creatures
on the Earth and deep in Seas
but also the souls of all people
in our planet
had lived from beginning of Time

suddenly to awake in the Day of Judgment
when even objects without souls
around us
like mountains, sun, stars
and heaven itself
will trembled, melted, converted and fell down

Upon the almighty signal
with the greatest, broadest and deepest
bandwidth capacity
and transformational power.

Zamir Osorov

http://www.amazon.de/Himalaya-Mountains-Kurzgeschichten-AmazonGlobal-bestellbar-Belletristik/s?ie=UTF8&page=1&rh=n%3A68079011%2Ck%3AHimalaya%20Mountains%2Cp_n_shipping_option-bin%3A2019341031

Pray for the West

Pray for the cursed West
communists, salinists, satanists, jihadists, chauvinists, islamists
and all others sorts of maniacs and terrorists.
Pray for the blasphemys West
all the wicked ones
and curved sort of people,
goblins and orcas
who dreamed about strong power,
dictatorship regimes and repressions,
who could not live
without mass violence and massacres.

You thought long time about fatal weakness of West
and democracy
and persuaded themself
about its miseries and impotence?
Ayatollah, who so long saved in the West
and returning to Iran cursed West.
Eduard Limonov, another terrorist
who saved by the West from USSR
and later also cursed and despised his savior
and many, many others blockheads
and traitors of freedom.

You are all who despised and hated the West
pray for West
and asking forgive for themselves.

What you will do
if the West tired deadly from worlds ungratefulness
produced the great warrior
like a new Alexander the Great?
Yes, what you will do -
all sorts of terrorists with clock bombs in hands
if the new president of USA or Germany
stopped the endless discussion
and joined all the West powers
or gone himself with war against you?

How you saved yours countries and survived
if the truly giants and colossus of our realm
suddenly lost tempers and announce a new Crusaders launch
against worldwide terrorists and fanatics?

Where hidden ayatollahs, national lieders,
post-communists, post-fascists
and all other kim chen yres, nasrales and dwarves
when Alexander the Revenger gone against you
and decided to crash all rotten and evil powers,
faked democracies for the thief and stealers
and sexually abused imamates with caliphates.

So I am asking you pray for West
and let the West
left forever with soft and delicate power

who trying helped to everyone,
who afraid own woman
and invented various stupid and naïve thins
like Magna Karta, Human right and other trifles and nonsense.
Let Obama played with that games
carefully and diligently
while you make own businesses and deals.

Just imagine what happened in the World
if instead him come to global power
not someone like president of North Korea
or Russian Federation
but one who really remained the great antic hero
who will able to tempt and arise the Western people
for the world war against fanats and terrorists.

Where you are all hidden
from his total and wholly superiority?

http://www.amazon.de/s/ref=sr_pg_3?rh=n%3A52044011%2Cn%3
A66034011%2Cn%3A67216011%2Ck%3AEmpire+Falls&page=3&
keywords=Empire+Falls&ie=UTF8&qid=1411877497

Between "falls in love"
and "falls empire"

My book has found place in category "falls in love" with the various items, handbooks and lore dedicated for the art of attraction truly love. Their titles very vividly expressed their content.

For example

How To Attract And Marry A Good Man:
What You Must Know To Attract, Fall In Love And Marry A Good Man

or

Attract The Right Girl:
How to Attract the Right Girls Effortlessly and Fast (Fall in Love Smart and Easily)

or

Falling In Love While Pretending to Fall In Love

or

Fall In Love and Stay In Love Forever:
It is like magic when you do it

My book looks consistently but nevertheless little oddly in such environment

Eleanor Rigby

The chronicles of great love and fall of great empire

How you like it? It sounds very ambitiously and provocatively isn't that? It reminded me about the worldwide famous and staunch motto of Communist party of USSR. While all other parties in the West called themself as right, left, middle, social-democratic, moderate Christian, conservator or republicans and so on the Communist party proclaimed itself as one along who have right to represent the voices of all people and protect their right. And how you like it motto - The communist party is the honor, pride and glory of our epoch.

After such historical reminiscence maybe had been better if I also give for my book more detailed short and additional explanation under the headline like

How to attract love, that you have seen in dream since the early youth

or

How attract marvelous girl from the other continent with whom you never meet before

or

The art of surviving in the telepathic surveys and hunt

or

How win the heart of west woman from high society if you born in developed country and no belong to elita and have not way to go abroad

or

How to win the best girl from the west and break out the all obstacles and barriers including the evil empire who trying to stop you

http://www.amazon.de/s/ref=sr_pg_3?rh=n%3A52044011%2Ck%3Afalls+in+love%2Cp_n_publication_date%3A183073031&page=3&keywords=falls+in+love&ie=UTF8&qid=1409249433

http://www.amazon.fr/Great-Falls-Livres-anglais-%C3%A9trangers/s?ie=UTF8&page=1&rh=n%3A52042011%2Ck%3AGreat%20Falls

The Japanese dream of Kyrgyz politicians

One day our politicians and generals fell to sleep all together and dreamed that woke up and finds ourselves, - where do you think? - on the island of Japan. In this wonderful country there people have no idea about corruption, nepotism, bribe and others innumerous sorts of lawlessness so familiar for us and our governments.

It was a very uncomfortable morning, I tell you, because our lieders and rulers under the sun of freedom and openness immediately felt themselves completely naked and defenseless.

Before they are coming to senses and understanding there they transcendence, in front of them appeared the journalists from the newspaper "Mainichi" and "Asahi", surrounded Kyrgyz politicians and began to ask tough questions and to ferret out and sniff everything and do it all very professionally, quickly sorting out, who is who and what s mean in our politic, what he worth and what sorts of mistakes and sins belonged him.

And then all these going to published in newspapers, showed by TV and paneled in on-line regime, through internet.

It produced effect of explosion for Japanese community. Our governors have appeared in front of a worldwide audience as they are and all informed, how our deputies and officials stole budget money, how they bribed by president and international organization, how they sold waters, gold, coal, pastures, forests and others resources. Also public became familiar with all the details of their personal life.

As a result, the ruthless prosecutors and investigators starting to hunt for our politicians, run after them, caught, sentenced and imprisoned them, and our leaders have bogged and stuck from head to toe in crimes and corruption: every deputy and minister was convicted for stealing money, bribes and kickbacks for the sale of land to foreign countries, for the adoption anti-state laws, the bill against common interests, when officials earn millions and some highest person even billions for the well hidden treachery acts. But playing such tricks were absolutely impossible with Japanese. Not only big machinations even the bribes and stealing's much more modest, like a hundred dollars stolen – all this cases found, registered and recorded precisely by the Japanese judges in the volumes and volumes of criminal books and presented as new and new articles of accusation.

As a result of such very fruitful and honest investigation all our politicians were sentenced to the life imprisonment, some of them got several such sentences. For example prime-minister who sold water resources has been penalized for 10 life imprisonments and president who prepared papers for selling hydro-electro plants and resources for 20 lives.

The deputies of Kyrgyz Parliaments who just voted for decisions, sentenced for 2-3 lives imprisonments.

In order to somehow solve this problem, the Japanese parliament towards our politicians endorsed historic decision, which allowed save faces for all our political criminals. Japanese kindly offered to our officials instead of serving life sentences in prison, going through ritual of last cleansing called hara-kiri. Because it was the only way for Kyrgyz politics to wash up the all dirty and crimes which they made and just after that the future of their descendants should not suffer from enormous crimes and sins of their fathers an predecessor's

But our politicians have not any idea about samurai Cod and honor and, therefore, shocked to death from such suggestion, they preferred to stay life-time in comfortable prisons there. But Japanese relates imposed them to take such a rite of purification. It appears, as determined Japanese prophets, the sins of our politicians are so great that only the mass hara-kiri's without exception could help the Kyrgyz politicians save their images and faces.

What started here, I must to say, the end of the world! Every day at the central Plaza of Tokyo Japan justice went our deputies and officials and forced them to make a hara-kiri in the name of cleansing their grievous sins. Most cry and beg the Japanese government and emperor to be given to live in a Japanese prison, but the descendants of the samurai were relentless and sincerely worried for the future of our country. Because just after such severely punishment our country and people could find hope for better life.

They brought our politicians to the place of execution, give them into the hands a sharp knives and forced to do hara-kiri, helping to those who could not do it.

Usually samurai waited less than a minute until the Kyrgyz official tried to kill himself cutting stomach, and then, if the official did not dare such a feat, the samurai himself stabbed them.

When all our politicians have gone through these terrible trials, they also woke up together in the next world, to go to hell - and the same Japanese hell, imagine.

There they were met by a terrible demon-saucy who said that our politicians in the hell ought to repeat this procedure of hara-kiri many-many times. When deputies soul cried out - how much it can last, the demon replied coolly, giving them a dagger - until the Kyrgyzstan could not completely repaired from theirs sins and not reached the prosperity and welfare as Japan.

But then... the deputies suddenly woke up from this nightmare, with the great joy realizing that all iust had dreamed them and there is no sulfur hell, no strong responsibilities - they are all lived in the most beautiful country called Kyrgyzstan, where quite possible to live happy and steal, and betray and sell the country, and none for that call you for answer, not put in jail, does not require you to be on the same day made a hara-kiri.

And if should come eventually the day of Judgment and prosecutors calling for answers... what to say about it, it would not be our headache, care and song. Our people and politicians don't like many thinks about such sorts of things.

http://www.amazon.co.jp/s/ref=sr_nr_i_0?rh=k%3Apartridge+sing apore%2Ci%3Aenglish-books&keywords=partridge+singapore&ie =UTF8&qid=1412307058

The serpent patron

Occasionally I have seen in dreams a snakes, sometimes with the most incredible colors and tones: orange, pink, dark-blue, and even dark crimson, with the metal tint along the back. Invariably of plots and details of such visions I am evoked with fear and terror, interwoven with disgust and I thought such feelings would share with me almost all inhabitants of our planet, even those who preyed on snakes as for a favorite food.

While some experts believed that snakes very useful and not so aggressive and insidious as they seem, some person even convinced that they are very affectionate and friendly, nevertheless, if you just imagined that in your garden, under a bush or under the wooden floor of your bedroom might to live cobra or viper... In short, you know what I mean and feel...

There are existed different hypotheses about this subject, but still scientists didn't know get convincing answer to the question: "Why are we so afraid snakes?'

Why even such meeting in dream so shuddered and stressed us, when even in our dreams the snakes behaved independently, with dignity and friendliness?

As we said early most others animals also have shared these our feelings, especially mammals and birds, even those which feed on reptiles, before attacking the snakes, overcome the instinctive fear and dislike for these kind of creatures.

It goes without saying that a separation between human and many other inhabitants of our planet and snakes rooted very deeply in past and nothing to do with. It's very difficult to recognize in these creeping creatures our distant legless and handles relates and brothers.

And the fact that snakes give us a poison, which saved thousands of human lives from specific diseases every year could not change the matter as the fact that snakes are hunting and terminated mice and rats and others very unpleasant and dangerous creatures.

Evidently we need for much good reasons and backgrounded events, to change our attitude towards snakes.

Perhaps this separation and confrontation will keep and going so long until we meet in future in the far corner of universe the other civilization much more advanced and reasonable compare with ours but which originated from the snake-like species and primarily loved and saved us from calamity and we answered them eventually with gratitude. Maybe after that we gradiently rehabilitated our terrestrial snakes as well. Of course, if we do not wipe them out till that time.

But that is a quite different story. Today I want to look to "snake" problem from a one angle and point of view – Kyrgyz traditionally attitude.

The bottom line is the next the dream when we have seen snakes belonged to happy ones, bearing good sign and most fortunately for our people, even more happy and hopeful than a dream in which we might to fly, ascend to heaven.

What is the reason backed such belief I don't know but I remembered my joy when I learned about existence of such sign and immediately believed them, because the snake dreams freaked me often before, and I was very glad for such conclusions.

Really such signs and believes are not taken in empty ground, they grown up from generation to generation, coming to us from the deep past. Especially pointing the fact that meeting with the snake, even in a dream, it is always a serious test. But when you wake up and realized that it was only a dream, and besides, one of the happiest and promising dreams – you filled with the best hopes and waited subconsciously a new discoveries and breakthroughs that never failed and disheartened you.

The more scarier snake you have seen, the more greater effect and reward prepare and wait for you. And immediately the horror and fear by meeting with snakes changed for the inspiration, hope and gratitude. Over time you start to fall in love with these dreams and even flirt with the snake motives.

For example, recently I had a dream (though it was not the deep sleep, I suspected that slept) and sow snakes - and was not afraid of them. Looked in their eyes, which had a lot from female eyes and my joy was not completely selfish. I admired them, not thinking about my profits and hopes - just accepting another mystery of our subconscious and nature.

Even if the Kyrgyz sign about snakes in our dreams is no more than a myth, a free fantasy, and then there is absolutely no mystery, however, such idea seems created from the extremely humanistic position to the person, and to the snakes, as if suggested by the highest wisdom, that try to set out, reconciled, united and blessed all sides.

And by the way, as shown the psychoanalytic studies, those persons who have had contacts with the representatives of extraterrestrial civilizations, parallel worlds and other forms of reality clearly witnessed that alien minds gently dealing with limited human consciousness, tried to slightly increase its natural features and perception, with the suggestion to him bright holographic pictures, unusual thoughts and associations, and testing them with the same snakes motives.

All these people who were on the verge of, or beyond, glancing at the surrounding reality through the eyes of a more highly developed beings have experienced at some stage, emotional stresses and fears, akin to that senses which we feeling when seen snakes in a dream or reality.

Supposedly, the high intellects which are invisible surrounding us intended and motivated for our fast overcoming such kind of fears. Perhaps it is one of the basic conditions for the starting dialogue between civilizations. So with the snakes better not to joke and respected them - in the earthly and cosmic sense and context of this word and matter. As said Arthur Clark our universe very old and reptiles, certainly, much more older and keep more mysteries than human beings.

http://www.amazon.it/s/ref=sr_ex_n_1?rh=n%3A433842031%2Ck%3Apartridge+singapore&bbn=433842031&keywords=partridge+singapore&ie=UTF8&qid=1412568520

http://www.chapters.indigo.ca/home/search/?keywords=Eleanor&langtype=4105&facetIds=528239|#ageValues%5B%5D=8&ageValues%5B%5D=18&facetIds=561001&page=0&priceValues%5B%5D=0&priceValues%5B%5D=20&sc=&sf=&sortDirection=1&sortKey=sales_retail_30days

Remembrance about Turkey

and dear friends Douglas Bruce and Marie Claude
so kindly invited us to Bosporus

Ataturk had been really the great man who equaled to Lee Quant, Mannerheim, Mahatma Gandy, Relay Jeanne and other reformators, lieders and founders of nations in our history.

I have ranged him to more high position then even Piter the Great and incomparable with such "great historical persons" as Lenin, Stalin, Tamerlane, Chingiz khan, Alexander the Great and many-many others the most energetic and influential persons in history. Why and on such ground I have got such belief?

Because we have seen today - almost hundred years later after his leadership and life - the real fruits of his politic - this fascinating, growing and prosperous Turkey governed by invisible hand of democracy and free economic. Look what was happened with previously maybe glorious in surface but mentally bad and deeply suffered Ottoman empire, the European ill man? Instead of long termed militaristic and expansionistic life-style, we have seen bursting economics, unleashing human initiations, social various and malty-level potencies and these tendencies got the deep changing in nations mentality – changing from aggressiveness to friendliness, from closeness to openness and kindness, from obsessing with states values and prerogatives to family values and human rights. Never before for the thousand years of history of

Osmans the lives of Turkic children and their future have been such well protected from wars, calamities and others disastrous as now and never before the present and fast looming future of country have been such promising for young generation from the point of great scale of real and multiple choices, expectances and hopes. Never before the mothers and fathers of these happy offspring's have been in such degree well educated, careful and kind and tend as now.

Thats why Ataturk was really the great person in worlds history.

He did the next things that are really important for the future of nation:

1. Turn Turkey from Islamic state towards secular democracy and parliamentarism, used strong power and personal authority for reaching this long termed aim, did everything for unavoidability such historical perspective for Turkey. You might imagine how utterly difficult had to do it when remembered about Islamic leading role of Osman empire in many centuries, the many generation of its sultans carried out the title of Halif (equaled to title of Pope in Christian world).
2. Changed nation mentality from position on eternal enemy of Europe to the integral part of this subculture. Before Ataturk Turkey eight hundred years identified itself as a strong enemy of Europe civilization as its primary rivals and sometimes conquerors and "Gods scourge".
3. His reforms in Turkic language had been aimed for joining with others Turkic nations in the Eurasian subcontinent and helped to integrate all Turkic world and involved them - in the first phase to establish modern Turkey and the next – to help established others Turkic states and nation as it

happened right now when Turkey as a modern train pulled other turkic nation in the well protected future.

But not all so simple. Turkic society today left deeply polarised between seqularists and islamists and from interim government existed real dangerous for the Turkic democracy. This great country again utterly need for the new Ataturk who will able completed the victory of democracy in Turkey. Yes, not plying with democratic inctitution for the gain short term advances but creating strong base of political freedom and strictly fanctioned sistem of election and renewing and changing incessantly the political elites of Turkey.

No any rotten tomatos.

The city for sea birds

Istanbul is the great city
with astonishing past, modern present
and marvelous future.
no one has argued
such compliment.
Also Istanbul very convenient for nesting and resting my favorite
various birds
seagulls, typhoons, albatrosses, cranes and storks
on the multiple round caped mosques with minarets
and others high and broad stretched to heaven buildings.
Not only overseas ornitas
the people who lived in hotels
with restaurants in the tops
after having fish and drank wine
looking on excellent panorama of ancient city
dreamed about flying above Istanbul

as a happy end and finitas.

About loudly crying Istanbul's muezzins

That loudly dreadful and desperate cries
exploded horrible by the modern acoustic devises
sounded frantically as a clear witnesses
about not having any chance for being heard by heaven
with the such sort of prays and revives.
But Istanbul is beautiful and attractive
and its polyphonic namaz not erupt me.

Another one my religion

I believe to Swiss
that survived right in the center of Europe
confined by the powerful nations
that twice dropped
our world to chaos and confrontation.
In the last century

But Swiss escaped from military tempting
and from heavy pressure
of fashists from north and south -
going safely towards the prosperity
firmly handle neitralitety,
protect country
with the well-guarded border
with the strong spirit of independence,
with the well trained army
with the perfect knowledge,

and the perfect optics
and the perfect banking systems
with the strong guaranties
of safety your money
from inflation and others disastrous.

I believe to that country
based so strong, holistic and prosperous
much more than to others holy plays and seven wonders.

http://www.amazon.com/s/ref=sr_pg_2?rh=n%3A283155%2Cn%3A17%2Cn%3A10300%2Cn%3A10307%2Ck%3Agreat+love&page=2&sort=relevancerank&keywords=great+love&ie=UTF8&qid=1413649673

Maria might change the course of worlds history

Dutch frustration with Russia in the wake of the MH17 crash is taking on an increasingly personal note, as some called for Vladimir Putin's daughter to be deported from the Netherlands.

Pieter Broertjes, the mayor of the city of Hilversum, used a radio interview on Wednesday morning to call for 29-year-old Maria Putin, who is said to live in Voorschoten with her Dutch boyfriend, to be thrown out of the country.

More than half of the 298 people killed when the Malaysia Airlines plane crashed in eastern Ukraine last week were Dutch.

Broertjes later apologised for his remarks via Twitter, saying they were "not wise", but adding that "they stemmed from a feeling of helplessness that many will recognise".

A plane carrying the first 50 victims of the crash is expected to arrive this afternoon at Eindhoven airport, from where they will be transported to army barracks in Hilversum. The Dutch government has declared Wednesday a day of national mourning and will mark the bodies' arrival with a minute's silence across the country.

Ukrainians living in Holland have also called for a peaceful protest outside Putin's daughter's flat, according to De Telegraaf newspaper. It published a photograph of the apartment complex where Maria is said to live alongside the article on Monday.

Very little is known about the Russian president's two daughters, Maria and Yekaterina, who are completely sheltered from media attention and have never been officially photographed as adults.

But there have been persistent rumours linking Maria with Dutch citizen Jorrit Faassen. Dutch media claimed that Putin visited the couple last year, something his spokesman denied.

Faassen has held senior roles in the Russian firms Gazprom and Stroytransgaz, a pipeline manufacturer.

But maybe Maria has helped now to change the tragic course of Russia if she tell to her father:
"Dad, please stop what you done all these years - secretly fighting with West and Democracy. They are only had to support us in hard days for Russian state. How you no understand that such things as sovereign democracy not exist in nature!? If you want create lawfull society and state you must based on law - not for the loyal friends and favoriets and bribes for their supports. Who among yours close friends now - North Korean Kim Chen Yn, Syrian Bashar Assad, Belorussian Lukashenka and horridly killed Muammar Kaddafi and Ceausescu?!
Please, father, learn from West what to do and do that while we have not lost forever all hopes and possibilities for better future and hope of Russia and World and personal safety".

The remembrance about an old man who came to help us in cold winter

My book ranged with works of experts of civil society those long time learned the Central Asian temporal problems and hopes and searching ways leading for better future.

It was a snowy winter day in 1997 year when I firstly met with Frederick Star on press-conference in media-center AKI-press. This old man came to Kyrgyzstan from USA to help us, support our HGO sector and generally common activities in our deeply depressed region. Yes, only strong civil society might to help people and protect them from cold, unemployment, conflicts and others disasters. But that truth reached to our people slowly especially when it opposite by governments body that was greedy for money and corruption and poisoned by post-soviet nostalgia under the heavy influence and total dominance of Russian media and TV in our informational space.

Certainly some powerful forces and gamers of big police in Middle Asia hated such initiations long time before West pursuing, cultivating and nurturing quite different strategies and aims in Kyrgyzstan. I thought this book "The Politics of Chaos in the Middle East" de Olivier Roy (1 janvier 2008) and others similar independent works and investigations have given us the best tool for understanding what happened in our early years of freedom and what proceeding now.

"The Battle for Hearts and Minds - Using Soft Power to Undermine Terrorist Networks de Alexander", T J Lennon (3 octobre 2003)

"After the Czars and Commissars: Journalism in Authoritarian Post-Soviet Central Asia" de Eric Freedman et Richard Schafer (15 juin 201

"Civil Society in Central Asia" de S. Frederick Starr, M.Holt Ruffin et Daniel Waugh (1 juin 1999)

That books and many others exellent sources about our region you will find there:

http://www.amazon.fr/s/ref=sr_st_relevancerank?keywords=Civil+society+-+Asia%2C+Central&qid=1407030180&rh=n%3A52042011%2Ck%3ACivil+society+-+Asia%5Cc+Central&__mk_fr_FR=%C3%85M%C3%85Z%C3%95%C3%91&sort=relevancerank

I believe to Switzerland

I believe to Switzerland
that survived right in the center of Europe
confined by the powerful nations
that twice dropped
our world to chaos and confrontation.
In the last century

But Swiss escaped from military tempting
and from heavy pressure
of fashists from north and south -
going safely towards the prosperity
firmly handle neitralitety,
protect country
with the well-guarded border
with the strong spirit of independence,
with the well trained army
with the perfect knowledge,
and the perfect optics
and the perfect banking systems
with the strong guaranties
of safety your money
from inflation and others disastrous.

I believe to that country
based so strong, holistic and prosperous
much more than to others holy plays
and seven wonders.

Mother Ashirkul from Nooken, Kyrgyzstan, Central Asia

Life is a Bridge of Sighs over a river of tears like a pray
In the wind you plant your tears - the storm will blow them away
"Tears On The Wind" A-L Andresen

My mother Ashirkul was born 1932 at Nooken village, south part of Kyrgyzstan.

Her father, my grandfather from mothers side Kyrbankul had been wealthy and peaceful farmer, he not participate with his brothers in civil war and collectivization received as unavoidable step and present all his sheep, horses and cows from his pastures in Dobo Mazar to the found and support of collective farm of Nooken, later called as Rachmanjan.

Nevertheless in 1937 years he and his brother had been repressed atrocious as the enemies of people and Sovet rule, albeit they really helped to sustain collective farm.

So my grandmother Cholpon left with my 5 years mother and with the sons Subankul and Abyl, Begmat and Oskonby.

When started World War II Subankul and Abyl 18 and 16 years boys had been recruited to the front. Mother had been in that time 9 years girl and till the last days clearly kept in her mind the tragic events of her early childhood. Both elders sons of Cholpon did not return from war. One of them has been wounded to leg and then no letter received from both

159

Grandmother Cholpon waited her children until her death in 1947 years. She was just 35 years old. My mother in 15 years had left as orphan.

1950 year she married to Arzymbek and in 1953 year burn their first son Kalyinur, after two years second son Zairbek. I was born in 1957 year - the 3th of their son. After me my parents had a dotter Zinat (born 1959) and two little sons Nariman (62) and Bolot (1968).

My father Arzymbek Osorov in 1968– 1985 years worked as Communist party local lieder in various districts of Kyrgyzstan. 5 times elected as the deputy of Kyrgyz Republic Parliament

In 1995 years Abdrasyl aba, one of the elders of our Nooken village and participant of WWII before dying the next year called me to himself and revealed that brothers of my mother not been killed in war. According his witnesses they had been prisoned by the Germans soldiers and after end of war left in the Western zona of occupation. Abdrasil ava run from germans prison in the end of war and he said that one of the son of Cholpon Subankul or Abyl can not run with him frightened to be repressed as the son of enemies of Soviet who was been prisoned by germans and also he deeply worried about the safety of families left at Kyrgyzstan and didn't want to returned to USSR after end of WWII. Abdrasil aba kept this secret all his live frightening for his live.

In any case my mother waited his brothers all his live and never believed for their death. In 1970 years I am remembered as she told me about her dream where one of his brother returned at home - "he came to me on the great ship from the far and big country. haged me and told, dont worry, dear sister, from now and onward our life goes with happy treck."

Mother waited his brothers all her life but, alas, they can not to her and nor sending any letter.

Nevertheless I know firmly that my two uncles Subankul and Abil (or one of them) after WWII left in the WEST. Married there and lived with highly probability in USA but also maybe in Germany or emigrated to others western countries.

Certainly today they are maybe died but left their sons, children and grandchildren.

So dear westerns friends, if you know some information about Abyl and Sybankul sons of Kurbankul from the Central Asia, Kyrgyzstan, district Nooken, Dobo-Mazar please answer me and help find my relatives. I could not do that when my mother had lived but I must do that and find my lost uncles and their offsprings.

http://www.rakuten.com/sr/searchresults.aspx?qu=Eleanor#qu=Elea nor&con=1&from=6&page=9

Eternal "Eleanor Rigby"

in rock and classical music and literature
and in the heart of Central Asia

The first time I heard "Eleanor Rigby" through Paul Mauriat orchestral composition. I fall in love to this "classical sounding" majestic music, something from Mozart or Chopin as I thought. Late when I informed that it was again "Beatles", which created the "Girl", I was been really shocked and cherished forever by the quartet from England as the 16-years boy from Central Asia.

http://www.veooz.com/videos/20EmJx.html

On prime time of Amazon

Really? All the world, the best part of it, who read the books and loved the Beatles turn opinion to me? I am completely gobsmacked from such attention and honor.

But what can I do for all of us how save your interest? It was much easy if I have been the talking ape, potato or Martian or one who know technically how accumulate and ride the tsunamy of money.

Extraterrestrial verses

Why you have tried
write on English
so stubborn and ugly,
when you
do it much better on Russian
and Kyrgyz?
I don't know why,
but I am firmly believed
we are all living in such cracked time and epoch
that so terrible need
for the right - face to face talks,
and massively contacts and relations
with other side of our planet
still practically unknown for us as the back side of Moon.

Yes, we are all
West's and East's mere inhabitants
still separated awful and skilful from each others
and segregated by cold war traditions and rules.

So you are all,
dear westernians,
please receive me
and my verses
as a chimps trying to tell you,
as a raw letters from outlander,
as a sending signal from extraterrestrial world
suddenly come you unknown from where
that strongly motivated
for communications, deals and relation,
and have right for that
more them any other
missioner and peace makers.

Do you believe me
as a poor one
squeezed through Black Hole
and survived
for truly love
with broken soul and verses,
or you are preferred
to meet with excellent equipped terminators, translators,
mediators and hunters

from alien and hostile planets
who completely denied and hated you
and your way of life and ideals?

http://www.avoprime.com/search?&q=Empire&node=10303

Asking from Birke,
my people and hills

It is very strangely indeed
that our hills stretched one by one
upon long distances
from east to west
as a great tides
on far north have locked
with chain of blue majestic mountains
called (from left to right)
Kara-Tash, Tiger-shrine, Babash-Ata
Every one of them as high as Monblank
And longed together for 40 miles.
They are created excellent and elegant back picture
For the innumerous hills
Stretched one by one
From east to west
As a tides of great see
As it was specially designed
For creating the best skiing places,
For exercising center
To learning to fly with air-bicycles
For various type existing and non- evicting else
Wind-surfing, hill-serfings, slope jump and slope-glading
And others sports entertainments.

But much at all our hills convenient
For creating ideal stadiums
Of various sizes and models
For volley-ball, football, tennis,
For meeting and playing and singing
Surrounded by sea of poppies flourishing in spring

Eventually the day will come
when all that amazing tide-like hills
So nice looking in every season
And so convenient
For using as stadium, theaters
And others public commodities
In open air - to put in active turnover.
We just need add interim part
And do some preparation
So eloquent with
Nature plan and God wills,
So I doubt not
Our land transformed
For marvel country
Where collected the best poets and Gods messengers
around the world
To read poems, sing a songs
And praying for Glory of Heaven
And thousands of our Kyrgyz people
Filled that stadiums
On Birke hills
Singing with English-speaking guests
And praying with them
And poppies flowers dancing around

singing with people
And the best West Christian sendings
Risen up to heaven,
And angels above will singing with us
I am believing for that and asked for that
For the name of Crist and Wests advanced and truly Christian,
Let them invade and multiplying in our land
With our people who so long wait them
Lived so far from sea and ocean
Locked by great deserts around
Right in the center of Asia
The marvelous oasis of poppies
Because I love my Birke and wish it
Eternal life and prosperity.

http://www.lehmanns.de/search/quick?category=10&pubyear_from=2014&pubyear_to=2014&q=Eleanor&page=2

http://www.ceneo.pl/Literatura obcojezyczna;szukaj-Eleanor+Rigby

The tale about Mother and her Girl

(written on the base of ancient Kyrgys legend)

Once upon a time our mothers did not die at all. Yes it was happiest time when we are all lived together with our dear one... Our mothers lived with us, they were kissed us when we are felling to bed to sleep, before that were preparing in kitchen something delicious for our latest dinner, guided us when we gone somewhere or if we left them - found us and visited to us even if we have departed from her to another world. Yes, they found us for serving us with food in time, to take our worries, troubles, problems, illness and other calamities.

But those times long ago had pasted. And this tale about one of the most doleful and unhappest incident and lost in our history from that our Mankind could not recover and seems never will able to do it.

Remember.
Our lives are accelerating
year by year
century by century,
leaping from one epoch to others.
We have reach great
advantages and marvels
personally and commonly,

but not in the sacred venture
starting from early day of our family
when our mother kept us so tenderly.
You might gain all the world and marvels
but lost your mother you never find her again.

The story was telling to me from my mother and she heard it from her mother, my grandma - from her mother and so on. From generation to generation this solemn legend came to us from farest ancient times and moved toward a fares future.

There are lived a mother with her growing girl in one small mountain village placed in the slope of Kyrgyz Great Righe.

And what really has been very strangely in this history is the next evil fact: then more better has been mother by his native origin and parents servises, then worse has been her girl. It was very cruel coincidence indeed! You might dont believe me the girl totally dominated upon her mother as leader and more and more tyrannized old woman with her desires, demands, caprices.

The life of woman by the time changed more and more heavier - than more growing her daughter, then more growing her ambitions, demands and various heartless hobbits, games and tricks.

Once in the beautiful spring day she go up to the hill with her friends, other villager's girls. The weather was fine, hill covered with various and multiple flowers. The nice company was very happy, running in the top of hill, picking flowers, singing a songs and completely forgot about time to returning home and have dinner.

But mother didn't forget it. She came to girl herself with freshly prepared dinner in warm pot covered with shawl in her hands.

Girl even she want to eat, nevertheless exploded with angry when she look her mother with pot in her hands.

Who call you here!? Why on earth you came!? It would be better if you stand at home and wait when I return back! And who created you with such features! Look for others mothers, no one of them didn't try to be as you! They are all sit down at homes and satisfied with them, only you are pursuing me!

Indeed as it happened with some unbalanced offspring, her mother seems to her more cheaply and even ugly compare with mothers of others girls. But in reality her mother has been, as we said early, one of the marvels in the world, but she was been overfilled with love to her daughter and this feels frustrated and diminished her in the cruel eyes of her daughter that afraid lost respect in the eyes of her friends.

But in the next instant when her mother heavely go back, slowly ascending from hill, covered by pistachio trees, girl suddenly felt keen pity to her mother. Alas, such senses forgotten by girl as fast as mother vanished from wiev with her vexed condition and love.

Only mothers receive us as snow white and love even when we are dark as raven and when some of us look as a hedgehog completely covered with pricks they are didn't afraid to touch us warmly, believing sincerely that we are as mild as cotton.

In that time when happened what about we say, it was only one family has burdened with such heavy problems. In all other homes and families around and maybe in wholly world peoples and nations knew how to keep peace, love and tolerance in family attitudes.

But one little stone will able produce the great avalanche and calamity, and this unhappy story about very bad relation between mother and girl certainly could not last forever.

...One day mother is sharply outraged her daughter because her wearing was very poor.

- Why you bring these old rags? - shouted girl to her mother pointing her old blouse, socks, pullover. Yes, mother was wearied old wearing but she nevertheless has been neatly and cleanly look. In the same time girl herself was been wearied in completely new coat bayed two day ago in local market for the last money. Mother is bought for her all what she asked.

Mother saying nothing for such cruel sentences with lowered eyes she is moving close to the oven in the corner of room. Her poor head long ago suffered from ache, her heart broken from injustices, pains and undeserved attitude from own child, but she can not keep a hate against the girl as can do some modern strong mothers well trained and practiced for prepare severe lessons and testings for children as they are running out from their controls.

Girl played all the day and when come back to home in late evening and found home is empty. She discovered that mother was not at home now, and what it worse oven is cold and no one to intent prepare something to eat for her. But girl felt herself happy in that first day of losing her mother. She just didn't believe that there are could happen something calamitous. The next day she played all day firmly belived, that mother has gone to meet with relates, lived in other village.

But mother didn't return to home the next evening too.

In the third day also mother didn't return to home.

Eventually girl starting to understand that there are something awful happened with her and she decided to call her mother.

"Mother where are you? Please return to me. I will never more to cry to you".

Yes, for the first time in her life, girl felt that can not live without mom and that often did wrongly against the dearest creature in the world.

Then girl turning to the Heaven. She prayed and cried almost all night asking mercifulness from God, hoping that he could help her. Poor girl didn't understand that Heaven usually has helped people only in frame of carefully created laws and tendencies and only in exceptional cases go to break its universal rules, especially when asked person not holly man but one unhappy and nasty girl.

Close to the early morning girl felled sleep (or maybe it was a faint) tired from suffering and crying. And she sow a strange dream. Someone or something invisible in compete darkness asked her:

- Are you really want to return your mother?

And girl answered:

- Yes, I want it more than anybody or anything in the world. I will never treat her and disrespect more. I swear.

As she said the last word, outside the darkness vanished for instance from strong burst of lightning, and after that the thunderstorm stressed the world and starting rain.

(As you see providence help to us to find powerful and correct words when we have lot of trouble but, alas, we are often so forgetful and stupid just the next instant when peace and happiness turned to us).

It was a warm rain as tears of mother that poured to earth.

How beautiful morning came after it! Rain is stopped just in moment when new day was born and sun rose from green horizon. The hills covered with grass polished with heaven water also look as newborn, the myriads of various flowers flourished as prepared for grand fest

Yes, people also in that morning look unusual - refreshed and as they were newborn too. It was clearly for girl that all villagers prepared for some grand fest. She didn't now what is the occasion but felt that it has some attitude for her person too. And as you know she liked to spent time in the fests very much.

And she run to the fest from the top of hill where she lived with her mother in the spring yurt toward the backside of slope where in big fruit gardens people prepared for fest.

When she run outside she met her mother who as usual not only look with love to daughter after free days missing each others, but preparing for meeting with her she is collected on the hill delicious mushrooms grown so fast after night raining. Mother knew that girl very liked excellent breakfast prepared from spring mushrooms. But girl didn't want to kiss and hug her mother who looked very weak and tired. That seemed to her to be not convenient instant when she liked and want to do it. He run outside through mother's opening hopes and hands.

She ran very fast to fest - down the hill – across the sea of freshly opened flowers - run to there, where in the nice and big garden all villagers, her friend and relates, collected for some big fest. Where have set outside kitchen with big kazans (potts) for preparing dishing, where erecting place for sitting people, row of benches and plays for game around for youth and children and others fests utensils.

Then she run up half a distance she met old man with white beard who looked unfamiliar to her. The old man tried to stopped girl but she didn't want to spent time for talking with old man.

She runs ahead.
Suddenly girl heard the next words

-    Last chance is over!

She turned back and didn't find old man, he was vanished.

She look ahead - and suddenly heard the keen crying of women. What is the shocking metamorphosing!? The instant before no one in the world could doubt that she run to the fest. She even clearly heard the fares smiles and giggles of young men and girls, children. And suddenly all that vanished and drown in the desperate and awful women crys. These sounds, it seems, raised to the heaven and far around - reached and wounded all the souls around and in the world - strong, keen, merciless.

It was clearly and sharp sign that the toy where she so fast running really was the prepare for say last respect and forgive for dying and prepared it for bury in the local cemetery on the top of hill.

She understood her mother is dead and never returned to her.

That is the end of this solemn tale about girl who fasted to the finest fest but reached to the sorrowest entertainment in the world.

From that times our mother after dying never returned to us. It was quite and completely impossible task.

The truly belief

Belief to the Democracy
is a really one
mighty, intrinsic and crafty belief to God.

How we find it?
Jesus Crist to show up clearly that.
Who bears the good fruits of world police,
who comes to the help to weakling and suppressed?
Look for the cause and effects of world police
what have done and not
by the various countries and nations,
who and how acted and show itself
in the various events and situations,
and you unavoidable come to conclusion,
all western countries of Democracy
belonged to the God and leading with his recommendations and
demands
I thought the really image of God
is the image and deep sense, meaning and future of Freedom and
Democracy.

So you have got now
why the dark forces and wicked angels
so hate the democracy?
Because they wanted ruled by world

as our cleptocratic lieders
and others fanatic and atavistic persons of history.
So USA have blessed and oiled by God
for the reign in our world
and our prosperity and better future.
And we had expelled the USA military airbase from our Manas
trying to expell and suppress the God will.
Woe for all of us, forgive us and return his protection, God,
Invisible and invincible
as the almighty and creative hand of truly Democracy.

http://www.amazon.co.jp/s/ref=sr_st_popularity-rank?_mk_ja_JP=%E3%82%AB%E3%82%BF%E3%82%AB%E3%83%8A&bbn=52033011&keywords=chronicles+of+great+love&qid=1410323576&rh=n%3A52033011%2Ck%3Achronicles+of+great+love&sort=popularity-rank

I have looked the future of Kyrgyzstan in Japan

Dear Prime Minister of Japan Shinzo Abe san,

I am glad informed you that my book "Eleanor Rigby" published and now distributed worldwide by nearly 100 distributers from 30 countries, including Japan, where my book received friendly.

http://www.amazon.co.jp/ELEANOR-RIGBY-chronicles-great-empire-ebook/dp/B00L8IUWZG/ref=sr_1_1?ie=UTF8&qid=140 6434398&sr=8-1&keywords=Zamir+Osorov This is a story about love between youth West and East, about Kyrgyz young man and English girl, that had happened in the age of Cold War, when our world was been deeply separated and stayed on the edge of total self-distraction. The music of "Beatles" helped to lovers navigate each other in a dreamland and eventually they were find each other's and completely transformed this world.

The history of modern Japan, it's astonishing achievement after World War II, that is really one of the best illustration of the limitless human power and free society and practice of your country have had the great inspiring capacity for all the people and nation in the world.

For Kyrgyzstan and for all Central Asian states today exceptionally valuable to learn the practice of West countries, create various lings and bridges between our nations and cultures.

8

I had been in Japan in 2006 with official government delegation from Kyrgyzstan and had met with many Japan officials, entered to the government building and residence of imperator of Japan. Panoramic photography of Tokyo had taken from the window of Japan government building, when we prepared meeting with prime-minister in his cabinet. I used in my book this picture as the illustration for the marvelous dream-vision about fantastic future of Kyrgyzstan.

Japan had a great impression for all of our delegation and many helped to Kyrgyzstan since the first years of our independence. And what need to stressed especially, the Japan's economic help and support was been exceptionally valuable and turned for realization the strategic projects as the building interregional road between south and north of Kyrgyzstan, modernization of international airport in capital and so on. Certainly Kyrgyz people and government could not do the best in their relation with the country of Rising Sun. We just have not been ready to answer adequately for the great possibilities that opened for us through increasing Kyrgyuz-Jupan relations. Nevertheless I hope that our relation steeply change in a next decades and we are too going to the best future handling strongly the road map from the Japans great reforms and ancient history and culture.

Best regards,
Zamir Osorov, author of "Eleanor Rigby"

http://www.amazon.co.jp/gp/aw/s?i=english-books&k=Nothing%20Change%20Love&p_76=2227293051

For our love to Big Brother

- Do you really love and loyal for Russia and Big Brother
who returned again in Kremlin?

- Yes, - we have answered and supported our corrupt governors, -
we must expel US base from Kyrgyzstan and did that,
killed with own hand the magic hen lying golden eggs
and harted stronly the eagle who protect us.

But expelling US airbase from Kyrgyzstan
that was only the first step
in strategy of our Big Brother
for our new and complete colonization.

-Have you really love and loyal to Russia and Big Brother
who returned again in Kremlin?

After airbase
as advised us
pro-Kremlin journalist Alexsander Knyzev,

with stubborn attempt to shape our common opinion,

you must to expel US embassy from Kyrgyzstan.

Eleanor Rigby II: Extracts from diary of great love and latest comments

He has tried to prove
that US airbase after expelling
might deploying dangerously
for our independence and freedom
under the Embassy's building in Bishkek

So after expelling airbase,
for our loyalty and love for Big Brother
our government must do the same
with US embassy,
expel them from Kyrgyzstan
and all others alien embassies together
located in our capital.

And that was also no end.
another pro-Kremlin writer Dmitry Orlov advised

-You must expelling all international organizations, projects and
programs
worked in Kyrgyz Republic,
if we really want to be a free
according with Kremlin plan and prescription.

Eventually as dreamed Jirinovski
deputy of Russian Duma
and very influential politic,
we mast expelled themselves
from Kyrgyzstan and Yssyk-Kul
for our loyalty and love to Big Brother.

For our loyalty and love to Big Brother
we must expelled themselves to Hell

http://www.amazon.fr/s/ref=sr_pg_3?rh=n%3A52042011%2Cn%3A
81604011%2Cn%3A83649011%2Ck%3AGood+%26+Evil&page=3
&keywords=Good+%26+Evil&ie=UTF8&qid=1409384498

The Indian Sun of democracy

India together with Japan, Malaysia, South Korea and some other democratic states one of the best historical examples of what happened with the Asian nation under the strict and long termed cultivation of the values of free economy and democratic society. Not so long days ago India were successfully provided the biggest democratic election of new president of country in the history of our world with the free voting more than half billion people(!).

For Kyrgyzstan and for all Central Asian states today exceptionally valuable to learn the knowledge and practice of West countries, create various lings and bridges between our nations and cultures and EC community and India as the West oriented greatest nation.

(From the letter to "The Indian Express")

But the Indians practice and democratic breaktruth especially valuable for the Asian supercontinent and our Globe at all in order to keeping stability and peace worldwide. When nation and great country counted more that billion people (6 part of world population) coming to the free consensus and made their historical choice - it caused the greatest positive effect not only for Indians but for the all Earth, bringing to them hope, energy, opened the best perspectives.

Every democratic and prosperous country in our planet looks as the shining star - the sunny republic - that not only make happy its inhabitants but also bringing the light and warm for its neighbors - close and far. And Indians democratic practice and everyday function I might comparing with the really Sun burning in the greatest continent. And every such political events as the free election of new president of India marked the strongest effect for all world population and give impact for other nation, awakening them for the more better future.

http://www.amazon.in/s/ref=sr_nr_n_6?rh=n%3A976389031%2Cn
%3A1318170031%2Ck%3Agreat+love&keywords=great+love&ie=
UTF8&qid=1410239783&rnid=976390031

The tragic games between rulers and people

Look for this tragic dilemma:
either people have reached the real powers
and handled the weel of engine
or government done the same
wiped people completely out
from ruling, managing and controling.

Either nation harnessed rulers
through election, freedoms
and other democratic institutions and values,
either rulers slipped away again and again
from common monitoring,
hooked heavily country by its gills.

At first scenario your fate going gradually
for recovering and prosperity
maybe slowly, after some disasters and calamities,
discherishes and dishonesties
under the guide by community,
but never lost hopes
the people who harnessed powers.

In the second case
when government bodies
took powers on theirs hand
the unhappy country and people
drifted slowly and implacable
for the stagnation and dying
through killing freedoms and justice
in police, mass-media, election,
eventually fatally
all structure descended to repressions.
unjustice, wars, starvation, deficient
and multiple lacks and problems
so familiar for Soviet empire
in its 7O year biography:
theirs birth, increasing,
pride, glory
and total worthlessness
and bankruptcy.

Our world has kept many other tragic examples
of unfoldment the worthiest scenarios
Look for the North Korean regime
or what happened with Cuba
under the life-long ruling of brave Fidel Castro,
honestly say two thirdth of all nation and countries
can not to learn this art
for their government firmly harnessing.
They appointment person, presidents and prime-ministers
slip away from common control
leading with their atavistic desires are sordid and sinister.

God bless USA and West as whole
to be a good teachers for this world
that is the best advice that I told
for the mine and next generations
who don't want sacrifice their precious lives
for the bad and incompetent guiding at all.

The revenged swear

The panoramic view of village Besh-Moinok, south Kyrgyzstan. one of the remotest corner of country where born and grown Jolchuby who planned to live there with his passion from England

Kyrgyzstan has a thousand such beautiful little villages which have lived and survived in long termed depressive state caused from the chronicle incompetence, irresponsibility and impotence of local and central governments. We have such sort of appointed officials which not able at all for creating a good conditions for the onset of stability and prosperity in such fruitful base and land.

Similarly picture you could observed in Kazakhstan, Uzbekistan and others our post-soviet neighbors.

Almost a quarter of century various politics that coming to power one by one, promised us the best future and reforms. One have sworn with hand dropped on Constitution that will transform country to another Switzerland for the 10 years of presidency, second inspired us with the perspective to reach the Japan, thirst oriented us toward the Turkey. But any time after inauguration and national celebrity all ruptures ended up with the same results - reforms gone no far from fixing on the papers and asking money from international funds and after receiving the very solid donations the reforms got setback and instead a tendency for diminishing corruption, cutting injustice and expelling frustration they are all increased dramatically, reaching for the dangerous level.

Kazakhstan and Uzbekistan possible now stayed in better conditions compare with our total hopelessness according with our own historical memory and practice. They are lived too long under the one authoritarian lieder - Uzbekistan almost 25 years ruled by Karimov and Kazahstan by Nazarbaev. And their people coming to firmly belief that process of transition for better future might be come just with the dismissing of senesce comrades and election a new presidents.

Kurgyz people have not now such naïve privileges. Since the 90 years till now we three time changed the presidents, firmly believed that the next lieder would be better then resigned and unlucky one and life in country starting accelerate toward prosperity future.

But every time the process going worthier with every new president and revolution and every new governor looked now much worthier then his predecessor. As a result many our analytics and common authorities tired deadly from political perturbations and now more and more telling about fatal mistakes in our past pointing clearly, that instead revoults would be better if we were lived under the one lieder.

But such conclusions are incorrect. All the sacrifices of Kyrgyz nation and efforts have not been fruitless and useless like to split-splashes of water in glass.

Akaev came to power and changed Masaliev, because he was been in that time the best one whom believed the elite of nation. It was historical fact. Also Bakiev changed 15 years of Akaev regime, after intrinsic peaceful revolution of 24 March 2005 year. That was also unchangeable historical fact. People have believed to Bakiev and wanted to see him in power.

After tragically April events of 2010 year through bloody clashing between protesters and the government forces in the power came Roza Otunbaeva as the interim president. It was also the result of compromise of oppositions lieders. Otunbaeva as a president even with the interim status, nevertheless have been better compare with her predecessors. Eventually at 2012 in the election wined the Almaz Atambaev and his victory also have been clearly predicted.

Bur why after such revolutions and changes Kyrgyzstan could not ended with the system crises and fastly lost its revolution spirit and great mood for transition, reforms and fighting with the corruption and dragons of nascent dictatorship? Why the election of new president in Kyrgyzstan transformed for something liked the game "Win the presidency – steal the billions – run out from country".

I thought much about the nature and core of Kyrgyz police, about their greediness, miserliness and about their fatally inclination for treason, and now understood, even they are all severely judged by history as a national traitors and had to bear the great historical responsibilities for the such long period of crisis and suffers and corruptions, they all have a very small chance for their rehabilitation and softening the final condemnation. They are all ruled by country which go agead under the heavy pressure of Kremlin, they were all acted, behaved and ruled in Kyrgyzstan as the hostess of Kremlin.

Kremlin, as a many could believe to that in last time, all these years plying own exceptionally sophisticated and efficiently strategic game for the discretization of independence/ fredom and future not only Kyrgyzstan but all other countries around Russian

Thank for events in Ukraine and Georgia we received lot information about nature and core of Russian police and about own historical past.

Undoubtedly Moscow handled his imperialistic police in past, has done in present and will do it in a future and 80 percentage of Russian population traditionally will support such police. But such pressure could not to help to escape our governor from the heaviest historical responsibilities. They were all have been mere a naught as a political figures primarily and ended their carriers as the round naught.

Atambaev, seems, with the others parts of his command sheared the tragic fate of ex-president and argued with such future hoping evidently that life in final exile with the worldwide shame but with the billions in bank accounts had been not so bad perspective for him and his family.

But listen what forestalled unwillingly about such gloomy future his close ally and "reformator" Omurbek Tekebaev in his notorious inspiring and touchy speech in Ata-Beit cemetery in the day of bury the bodies of 90 killing heroes of April events in the 2010 year:

"If we are also from now and onward after such many tragically deaths and sacrifices for the better future of Kyrgyz nation will do the same things as the run ex-president, not stopped the corruptions and tear out the roots of dictatorship style of governing and terminate all sufferings and injustice, our own fate must been even more worthier and bitter than the fate of cursed ex- president Bakiev who shot own people and run out from country. We swear you before the holy corpses of our young men and heroes that we never will do such shameful things, we never turn back to the past times".

Give the nation the good chance, cursed brethren! Please get out from power as early as possible all sorts of authoritarians lieders and dictators! Get out to hell!

To Mark Zuckerberg

(Nowadays imitation for the poem of Toktogul
"What kind of mother was born such son as Lenin?")

What kind of mother was born you, Mister Mark Zuckerberg,
the founder of Facebook and Google?
You are not just for yourself great wealth and success gained
but for everyone who registered in you system or just touched with
you tools.
You play with your platform and stuff as with magic vane.
You have endeavored to transform our environment
for the society of unlimitedly success and wonders.
where even the last one and mediocre among mediocres
have a good chance to be blessed enormously and grossly
for the run away from a bands of robbers, goblins and orcas
and outnumbered great portion of loosers
for the tragic events of modern history confused and contused.
Thank you very much Mister Mark Zuckerberg
for the great aim, tendencies and overwhelmed trend
you name written with golden treads and fluctuated synapses
on the heaven of World Wide Web.

Tolstoy as the peacemaker and wise Elder for the all times

You cannot find man for comparing with him, and possible in the history of human civilization have not been another one more worthy for calling a genius than Tolstoy. Although he had a low opinion about himself and did not like to talk on this subject. After two hundred years as he born, his novel "War and Peace" recognized as the most outstanding literary work among the all time and nations. Second place belonged to the George Orwell's "1984."

About Julius Caesar, ancient historians wrote whatever he does, no matter what actions performs or decrees signs or just speaks or recommends in private talk – all his activities marked with the stamp of his truly genius.

Leo Tolstoy had not been a king, but for him the mentioned words have much more attitudes than to the Emperor of Rome. All his long life from beginning to end, in all its manifestations was been the life of a genius.

Until the last day, in the country where he born, existed common misconception about him. Many people sincerely believed that this man ended his life not very well as it worth for the great person, comparing his fate with the King Lears last days, who goes out from society, left the family, which called him as crazy old man, a maniac, even tried to build around him the theory about a degradation human identity over the years, and so on.

But now, a hundred years after his death, we suddenly began to realize that the last years of Leo Tolstoy – his old age – was been perhaps the most great and valuable page of his biography. Because, whatever did this "madcap and moody old man", all shining with the extraordinary genius and his wisdom and greatness but his contemporaries often could not seen that or did not want this, roaming in the mist of prejudice or in the compete darkness.

He distributed his land to the peasants, the fee from the sale of "Anna Karenina" directed for the support and evacuation from Russia to Canada the thousands "duchobors" - the Protestant currents among Russian Orthodox Church. He actively professed the philosophy of non-resistance to evil and violence.

He is infinitely perfect and profound in general and in details. For example, being himself vegetarian he advocated not only for the end of the terrible suffering any kind of animals that we kill for food, but also developed the early project of the Convention of the Rights of animals, which was created and adopted much later in Western Europe. And Tolstoy considered and counted justifiable to cultivate the same attitude and humanitarian principles toward the vegetables.

He condemned the cruel Chechen war started by Russian tsarist empire, ruthlessly exposing the brutality of Russian soldiers in his book "Caucus prisoner" though when he was young, he participated in Crimean war and showed himself as the hero in the battles for Sevastopol. He called the Orthodox religion as the misguided branch of Christianity, though revered and loved Christ more than anyone else. He was outcastes by the Russian Orthodox Church and anathematized. He opposed the war between Russia and Japan, and as we now understand in the twilight of his life, he tried to prevent a steady movement all Europe and the world toward the First world war, revolution and chaos.

Had he lived another 10-15 years, perhaps, our world could have been saved from a terrible impending disaster.

Tolstoy was been a truly Elder, the wise man for the all times as represented Kyrgyz people that title for the man who able to see the truth so deep and so perfect and say that so bravely to the people, kings, all over the world.

Read how mocked 90-years Tolstoy by the Russian patriots, that fanning the flames of World War I.

"Moscow Bedomosty" July 10 (June 27) 1904.

About Lev Tolstoy and his anti-War position

"Count Tolstoy now completely has alien to Russia, and for him is no mean completely whether or not the Japanese hold Moscow, St. Petersburg and throughout Russia, but Russia would soon sign a peace treaty with Japan, on what you want, even the most humiliating and shameful conditions.

So vulgar and despicable not feel, think, and speak any other Russian person.

Now he released abroad outrageous pamphlet against Russia, with whom he had finally breaks all ties. If he still lives within Russia, this is happened only from the generosity of the

Government of the Russian, still reveres former talented writer Leo Tolstoy, whom nowaday old maniac from Yasnaya Polyana and blasphemer have nothing in common.

If the government found it possible to rip the mask from Count Tolstoy and show the Russian people all hideous nakedness of his face and soul, then this would put an end to all our Tolstoy cult and then, but only then, could be given to old screwball the possibility for quietly live out their old days in his Yasnaya Polyana and bury there his former glory."

http://www.fishpond.com.au/c/Books/Fiction Literature/q/great+love?rid=2057751326&outprint=1&format=Hardback

For the favorite small West's countries

I found another company from Nederland and Belgium with office in Utrecht that has sold my e-book. I wish its staff the great success and if my book has sold very well I will be happy to make visit to that region of Europe that's famous as the cradle of democracy and freedom.

These small countries of the West together with Denmark, Sweden, Norway, Island and Finland have showed to us the lonely possible way for happy and prosperous future.

But, alas, we have not been the good students and lost many brilliant opportunities since the fall of Iron Fence. No wonder that after 24 years of such mediocre governing something like Iron Fence again to try to restore and separate our worlds and our freedom and independence fast shrinking and downgraded.

That's way I wish for the West the great achievements and the most spectacularly successes in all branches and entertainments and initiations. Let all other world understand and deeply believed that all nation haven't other alternative for surviving and prosperity than what have done this small European countries.

West has supported us
sincerely and honestly
planting seeds of democracy
and sustainable society
in our crude land,

but hearts of our people
still attached very strong
to old illusions,
and Kremlin genius
very artful and virtuously
played with our post-soviet nostalgias and syndromes,
pushing us back in USSR on and on.

We have hated our freedom, alas,
and greed for instant hot money along.
Humiliation not the word
tell me, experts, how long
this tragicomedy in 1/7 part of world prolong?

http://www.bol.com/nl/p/eleanor-rigby/9200000029873437/

http://www.bol.com/nl/s/boeken/zoekresultaten/N/2395+8292/
No/12/section/books/Ntt/great%2Blove/Nty/1/sc/books_en/index.
html?sort=bestverkocht_11

Heaven's mercy

(to Marie-Claude)

Suddenly
God helps me
to express myself correctly
and authentically
when we have sat on the sofa
in the luxurious guest-hall
lively but hardly discussion
about the values
of cultural influences
and interactions
between East and West
on the very bad tantalising English...

Suddenly my hand caught
the nice red pillow
in the shape of big human heart
among the various warm gears and toys
scattered on the sofa

and I said: "what I want to say

said for me this big red heart in my hand..."

overfilled with love and respect
to Swiss and German Ordnung,
stability and greatness
such astonishing
visualized
in the vast number of small neat and pretty villages
hidden in Schwarzwald.

Shophaim, 2011 years, august

http://www.lehmanns.ch/search/quick?mediatype_id=&q=eleanor
+rigby

The law of tenderness

The Kyrgyz philosopher and esthetician Begaly Tagaev in his 300 paged monografy "Naziktik temasy Kyrgyz adabiatynda"(Tenderness as esthetic category and its omnipresentness in Kyrgyz literature, ancient and modern) came to conclusion that our world and mankind find way to harmony and peace according to the laws of justice and tenderness.

Yes, John Lennon and Leo Tolstoy are right, we must do all to escape hate and war and turn to love.

Moreover, every living creature in the world and even any entity and any object, - even among them the tiniest and naughtiest - any phenomenon or manifestation of the objective and subjective world should be considered as unique and extraordinary things that require appropriate with reverent attitude, understanding and comprehension.

Than farther forward moving humanity, than more clearer, deeper and more fully had aware that one of the main obstacles to its development are the rudeness and sinicism belonged and coherent his nature, what was, saying more correctly, imposed to human by the imperfection of his existence - current and preceding.

Love me tender asked us all universe if you wanted to live happy and prosperous and protected from all sides.

The shortest novel about the grand evolutional story:
Little work with the great love

Lack of love

Our world overwhelmingly
need to love, not war
look, how strong and powerful acted
national lieder of Russia
as a man of lie and head of states of conflicts, plots, violence and hatred
who might this empire to stop
and his deep rooted evilness crashing?
Only great love to world, peace and Russian.

Look for the millions religious fundamentalists
who ready with name of God to killing innocent people
exploding skyscrapers and get down airplane
Who born this horde of murders and killers?
Only lack of love
toward the great number of nation
lived in the deserts bearing in ground
the sea of gas and oil
but so catastrophically
lacked inwardly and outwardly
from truly hope and love.

http://book.daum.net/search/bookSearch.do?query=great+love

Requiem for MH 17

Almost 300 civilians
who had absolutely nothing to do with war in Ukraine
between government forces and separatist
killed with surface-to-air missile
launched mistakenly from the place controlled rebels.
Among died - 80 children and 2 infants

The Boing MH 17 flew on the height of 30 thousand feet
from Amsterdam to Kuala-Lumpur.
Almost 200 Dutchmen, dozen Australian, Malaysian. Germans,
Britainians, Canadians. Americans
instead of summer vacation
fell down to crash site and their deformed bodies
two days decomposed under the feet of separatist,
who proceeded torture them afterlife,
stole their money, credit cards, golden rings,
turned up their bags,
while the grown international violation
not stopped these acts of blasphemy.

That was result of aghast confrontation
"sovereign democracy" and world of freedom and democracy,
the product of stubborn politic and efforts

for creating new Eurasian identity
of corruptive and cleptocratic states
on the post-Soviet area.

O yea, the Russian government
overwhelmed with imperialistic nostalgia
many years carried the war on its close borders
and far away from it
everywhere trying undermined
the tendency for stability and restoration.

This state governed by intelligent services
sophisticatedly and diligently
learned and prepared people for hate peace and stability.

O yes, their military men skilled perfectly
for targeting death carrying missiles
far above us to stratosphere.

So many people and children
killed by this geopolitical invention
In Chechenia, Syria, Georgia, Ukraine,
elsewhere in the world

As long before the Soviet Empire
in Korean peninsula, Afghanistan, Vietnam
everywhere where have access this state
of political radicals and terrorists,
they killed mercilessly people, freedom and prosperity
for the better future

Even now every day
one or two Kyrgyz young gastarbaiters
killed in Russia
and send in coffins to fatherland.

More than 300 hundred Tajiks
more than 300 Uzbeks
killed every year
in that no declared but real war
against ethnic minority, freedom and independence,
against prosperity and West influence,
against universal values
so distinctly and valuable
as justice, judges independence, election system
as priority of human rights
and right everyone for safety life

Who fights so long and stubbornly
against clear universal commandments?

Who points missiles to heaven
against nascent democracy,
future generation and the best experts of AIDS?

Who fight so selectively and concise
against surviving and prosperity for everyone
and world as whole?

You must condemn, jail and expel forever
those who pointed to heaven
sophisticatedly designed and merciless missiles,
How long will be rain from there
the bodies of men that had nothing to do with yours war,
the dissected part of children and their toys,
the hope of the world and peaceful folks for better and healthy
future,
where precisely worked the law of love and attractions
and no place for barbarity, cruelty and cynicisms?

Those who pointed death to heaven
must be fell from heaven,
with naked torso and trained body
(it would be fanniest photo session
of man who such obsesses with such tricks),
who dreamed so long about restoring evil empire
undermining everywhere the blessed move, trend and intention
for the freedom, democracy and happy future.

The daughter of Ocean

Written on the base of ancients Kyrgyz and Celtic legends

According to archaeological dates, four thousand years ago, Issyk-Kul lake was substantially less in size and containing scope of water than now. Ancient towns once flourished around not so big lake, as well as rich lands and pastures were there that flooded late, after the famous great earthquake described in many old sources and scriptures jerked the massively landslide whereby the channel of the river flowing from the lake was blocked by the stripped mood and fallen stones from towering mountain. As a result Boom and Chui rivers became shallow, and Issyk-Kul basin filled with water and took the same great and majestic shape that so familiar to us now.

However, in the past, everything was different, here on the vast lands that now covered by water was established one of the early civilization, which called and entitled in old books as the Aryan.

The story that describes here, occurred in this era, and wise readers themselves make sure and assess as far as author could be strict and impartial in description of the oldest events, that might cast bright light for our contemporary life and reality.

Once in those days and times, on the edge of deserted lake in southern, wild and remotest part of Issyk-Kul valley there is an young shepherd, the son of a single woman, grazed a small herd of sheep. Their house and yard were located far from water in the slope of surrounding mountain, but shepherd tended graze sheep close to the lake margin, on the hills covered with lush greenery that steep descended to the blue water. So it was an ordinary day close to its zenith when the young man would lie down on the grass and let himself forget about sheep, which also rested lying in grass well fed and there was no danger that they may be somewhere hidden or lost in the thickets of sea buckthorn on the edge or go further somewhere.

And when he was fell deep in thought about how beautiful this world and lake looking, how full of various sorts of secrets and magic they were, suddenly he hears a tender maiden song, which was reaching from the lake's side.

"What is that? Maybe, I dreamed or caught by some obsession?"- He asked to himself, and then rising from the green grass to full height and turned toward the Issyk-Kul.

To his amazement, he saw the girl slowly floating in the shallow water and singing a wonderful song. It seemed that she did not pay any attention and even notice the boy standing on the shore, but apart them there was no one soul in this hidden and remotest part of the vast valley.

Mermaid incessantly singing swam very close to the shore and climbed on one of the slippery, covered with algae large flat stones, by which so abounded the southern part of lake. She sang, turning his face to the sun and again to water, looking at hers reflection in the crystal clear surface, adjusting and combing long golden hair with fingers. From the wonderful song and voice of the girl it seems even songbirds hidden somewhere in the thickets of sea buckthorn, barberry and karagach-trees grove on the bank stopped their singings and voices for instance at all as if enchanted not less than shepherd by the song.

He went like in dream to the water's edge. She was so beautiful and unusual that young man not only lost his head, but also desperately began to planning and search way to win this miracle, catch its heart. He pulled out from his bag what there laid his mother. It was a freshly baked round bread. Holding this present in his stretched ahead hands he went down close to the margin toward singing girl.

But Mermaid, when the young man approached her, slipped from the flat stone into the water and swam away to a safe distance. Then, interrupting her song, she turned to the young man with the next words:

Тартуулаган токочун, боз жигит,

Отко бир аз катуу какталып,

Жарабайт мага мындай белегиӊ,

Сен дагы мага жакпадыӊ...

Then Mermaid disappeared into the depths of waters. Shepherd left alone on the shore of so huge and desert lake, swept by the terrible anguish, because he felt like all passionate kyrgyz that without this girl he could not to live in this world.

He stood long on the margin, hoping that she returned to him, but she didn't.

Came back to home late than it happened usual he closed sheep into the barns and told mother all about the extraordinary vision and asked her advice - how he could attract, bewitch or do something like that for the attaching to himself forever such beauty and marry to her.

By the way his mother was a wise woman and quickly understood what happened with her son and told to him: "Try not to lose your head, son. Love to the mermaid, beautiful witch, morning mirage, dream it always the hard matter. Much better have been if you fell in love and merry to the pretty girl, find here around the lake, not searching her into deep water".

But son don't hear such word of mother because was really hurt by Mermaid and nothing to do with.

"Well, let's turn to the point - told mother, - Perhaps, the answer lies in the words that she said to you. I will bake you tokoch upon low heat, so that the dough was soft, slightly baked, and when you go back to graze sheep on the shore of the lake, offer her this bread, let's see what she would say this time? Maybe this bread much pleased her?"

The next day young man was on the lake with the sheep early, than usually, he constantly looked toward the lake, and seemed almost completely forgot about grazing sheep. But Mermaid did not appear. He climbed to nearest green hill and again went down to the water, but she not seen. Before him stretched endlessly, dreary and gloomy expanse and limitless of blue water.

And just at the evening, when he was ready going to home, he last time threw a glance at the lake and saw her, floating near the shore.

The young man hastened to her, and coming close to the water, when between them remained just few steps, he pulled from his bag tokoch and handed it towards girl, begging her with his all appearance to bring this present and not go away.

Girl, observing him, turned to him with the song, contained the next words:

Белек кылган токочуң кам экен,
Сага дагы таң болдум,
Зиректигиң аз экен,
Сен мага жакпадың, жаш жигит…

After these words, Mermaid swam to the some distance from edge where water fast gained depth and disappeared in the lake.

But this time, the young lover remarked to himself that the girl smiled at him before vanishing. He took that as a good sign for himself and decided to do all for the reaching his innermost desires.

Returning home, he told his mother all as it was and asked her advice again.

The next morning mother baked tokoch, kyrgyz dough, prepared from the excellent flour mixed with honey, milk and crumbled pieces of nuts, such kind of delicious bread our mothers and grandmas are usually baked on holidays and traditional festivals like Noorus.

Thus, for the third time the young man came to the shore of the lake to meet his fate. Girl was not long to show herself at this time too. It was a raining early but late close to the midday weather is changed, as often happened at Issyk-Kul valley and sun came to power and lake, green margin and surrounding blue mountains and green hills began playing with all the colors of a nice summer day. But the girl is not seen very long.

And only on bright sunset, when he had lost all patience, and came up with the dark thoughts that he did not live in this world without this girl, he heard again the familiar song wafting from the lake.

Mermaid swam in the water, sang the wonderful song (the most wonderful song in the world), and when she swam close to shore, the boy handed toward her the gently baked bread.

This time she did not swam away. Jigit walked right up to her, stepping into the cool water, she took his gift, moreover they are holding the hands each other dwelling up to the green shore.

The young man immediately confessed to the girl that he can not to live without her and ask her to be his bride.

Girl, smiling, listening the words of young man, and he went on and on telling her that without her his life has no meaning, that if she refuses him, he immediately jumped into the water - in the deep backwater on the beach and put an end to life.

In the end, Mermaid agreed to him, but put to shepherd the one solid condition.

"I'll be with you always, faithful and devoted to you, together in happiness and in sorrow, even when you and your people gone through hard days had never been in the past, but remember that you lose me, if you raise three time hands on me without any reason and grounds".

Of course, the young man said to her, that it would absolutely impossible thing to him that he had not only never do that but even think about such matter, that she no need worry about, even if she was guilty, he would not raise his hands on her.

Then they parted, agreeing to meet the next day. Before stepping out into the water girl took off from their left foot elegant sandals, embroidered with the large pearl beads, torn one of the pearls and handed it to him, then she wore up again sandals and step down into the water and disappeared.

The young man returned home that day, happy and crowded with the brightest hopes, as never before in his life. Told about everything that happened to mother, thanking her for her delicious baked bread and showed pearl bead.

The next day he will come again to the shore, dressed better than usual as going to fest, as his mother recommended him.

Like yesterday he waited Mermaid very long. In the end, he so offended or even had angry, because Kyrgyz, especially from the coast of Issyk-Kul, quickly disturbed and came to wrath, so he even thought that Mermaid merely joked him. "Well, I'll show you - the young man thought to oneself - what the joker I am." - He climbed to the hill, which steeply loomed over deep water with the firm decision to rush out upside down and end his life.

And at the last moment, he heard a terrible cry:

-     Stop! Go back down here!

The young man looked around and saw on the shore a stately old man who looks as a king with three beauties besides him.

When the jigit came to him, a stern old man addressed him with the following words:

-     So you ask my daughter's hand? And who are you actually?

- I am Babashbek - replied the young man, - I was born here
  and grew up. And who are you, father?
- I am Kol Buudan ata. Father of all water on earth, the king
  and the god of rivers, lakes, seas and oceans. If you're
  worthy my daughter, I will make you infinitely happy, and
  there is no king in the world who will able to violate you
  and your people, but if you will unworthy - I stop to help
  you, and you'll see yourself what happens then with you
  and your people.

After such mysterious words Kol Buudan ata turned to his
daughters:

- But first you have to guess which of my daughters is your
  favorite?

The shepherd looked closely at the three girls, they were
all alike as twins, dressed the same as the princess and it was
impossible to determine which of these three beauties was the very
Mermaid, with whom he spoke yesterday. Losing hope and have
just decided to randomly select one of three beauties, the young
man looked down, and suddenly noticed on the foot of one maidens
the slightly ruined sandals which didn't have a one pearl bead. The
young man pointed his finger at the girl - and at the same moment
the king and two others girls disappeared from view, and on the
shore he left along with lovely Mermaid.

- Well, get to accept gifts from my father - said Mermaid –
  start to count as long as possible taken the deep breath.

The young man took a deep breath and began to count - one, two, three, four, five, six...

While he is counting from the water began to go out well fed and bred sheep, one after other and mix with its grazing sheep on the coastline hill. The young man in the same breath could count up to twenty - and became richer for 20 selected sheep. He himself had a flock of about 40 sheep, but they were not as well-fed and pedigreed like the coming out of the lake. Shepherd quickly realized that with such luxurious additional sheep, he will become very rich in the future. But the most surprising thing was to come next, when Mermaid closed to one animal and spread up the strands on it back, and shepherd saw that the thick wool of the sheep-merino contained the golden sand!

- Each sheep in her wool bears a lot of golden sand, they shake it when come to home, - said the Mermaid. - Now take a deep breath and count again!

The young man began to count again. At this time, from the water began to appear the chosen well-bred cows, gracefully swaying, one by one. Young man was more lucky and practiced and counted to thirty on one breath, becoming richer for the magnificent thirty dairy cows.

When he rested at little, she told him again start a new counting.

From water began to appear excellent horses. Shepherd was able to bring the score to 40 before he completely left air in the lungs, he became richer for 40 horses, each of them was a real treasure.

Thus, our hero not only won a red scarf, as have said Kyrgyz, but at the same time became a very wealthy person.

They returned together to his house and lived happily and carefree, enjoying all the pleasures of life.

However, this was only the beginning of amazing career of Babashbek.

He lived with a young wife many years in mountains, happy and peacefully, whatever he did, he gained success and was a very prosperous, they were born and raised three sons. Babashbek became very influential among his people. But it was only visible part of all blessings. Mighty Ocean, Kol Buudan ata, blessed not only a young family, but all his people, who lived in ancient Issyk-Kul basin. Peace and prosperity come to this part of the land. Not only hunger and deprivation got out from there, but also wars and invasion of enemies stopped at all. Everyone thought it was just a coincidence, but in reality, it was the work of a powerful patron of all water on the Earth, the merciful and almighty Kol Buudana ata, who thus supported his daughter and son in law.

As a result in the Issyk-Kul basin the most astonishing things and events are happened there, unheard before in the realm of ancient Kyrgyz Chigu. Country Aryans gained not only political independence, but also has going to be a very influential state in region and broader on the international area, some experts and politologs at that time even talk and predict about the possible revival of the Kyrgyz great empire.

While neighboring countries languished in barbarity, tyranny and enmity to each other, which were the coherent feature and characteristic of all stupid and authoritarian regimes, Chigu began to show its deep interest to the high standards of democracy and justice, were undertaking relatively fair elections, as for the freedom of speech it seems to be a flourished in that country. What's more the land of Kyrgyz became going to know as an island of freedom and even some writers believed that it was emerging the new Atlantis, as another perfect kingdom of Light, Sun, Democracy and Justice and Prosperity that existed somewhere far to the West. That was certainly far from the truth, but, nevertheless, a some grain of it presented in similar allegations.

Since Babashbek was a very rich man, for him opened gate, leading to big politic, he was chosen to local municipal government, and then to be elected to the parliament of the country on the party lists.

In short Babashbek Zholborsmazarov became a member of parliament of Kyrgyz kingdom and was therefore forced to take up permanent residence in the city Buranum that placed in the Chui Valley, which was the capital of the Ancient Kyrgyz kingdom.

I must say that at that time Burana, the state capital was a great prosperous city, and manners of people in those days were about the same as now, because man does not change much over time. Babashbek becoming the member of parliament, and his wife, although she was naturally blonde and did not look like the typical kyrgyz woman, nevertheless very bad communicate in the language of citizens. As a result, townspeople treated them as myrkas because both bad could speak the language at the city, and spoke only at Kyrgyz.

But Babashbek Zholborsmazarov put a lot effort to learn the language of the city, and always wanted to go wearing well ironed trousers and clean clothes, intended strongly to not show his provincial origin.

And Babashbek Zholborsmazarov was very proud with own life. He considered himself a great politician and a man, although, in fact, all his achievements, good luck and success were going from father of water, it was all the merit of Ocean, the effect of his bless and support.

One day Babashbek met with other members of his party at the Kureltai appointed for discussion to very important public issue, where he forced came up with wife. Mermaid don't want go there and need to say preferred no interfere to the deals of her husband but this case was exceptional and Babashbek and others deputies decided come with wives there, showing to public the respect of gender matter. And I must say this Kurultaj rise up the question how make the country richer. Deputies put the matter bluntly - how to reduce the cost of holidays, toys, funerals and other ceremonial events, which since ancient times have plagued Kyrgyz people, that was excessively wasteful in this regard. If other nations cut only a sheep or gout to hold a wedding or other ritual cooking's, Kyrgyz was made at least cut a cow or mare for such ceremonies. This tradition was criticized heavy, but no one dare to take urgent measures against or suggests a restrictive laws. Every time when raised initiation for the reducing the level of eating meat, among chigunians found out the ardent supporters of democracy who passionately argued that such step will going to the serious violation of human rights and therefore being lawless.

This time also meeting appointed to the economy of the people's money and protect the natural resources and environment, because forests and pastures also suffered due to excessive abundance of grazing herds and flocks on them, came to opposite conclusions. Deputies decided not take any action and leave everything as before, and let people own decide - to cut or not sheep, cow and horses on holidays.

After that, the Babashbek and others members of parliament coalition together with their spouses gathered in the hall for celebrations, where they waited by excellent and excessively prepared dinner in the best traditions of Kyrgyz hospitality, when tables simply burst with viands and exquisite meat treats, there were not only rousted lambs, fishes, partridges but also kazy-karta, sausage from young horse meat, not to mention various alcoholic drinks - in short, the campaign against gluttony and excess, leads to new excesses and gluttony. And one of the deputies who had a few hundred thousand sheep, lot of horses and cows and even joked with another tost by saying the following phrase:

To save our gracious pastures from erosion
and forests from destruction,
must be cut as often as possible our cattle
and eat them lot.
More we eat them
the easier would be for our pastures.

And at a time when one of the deputies said fiery speeches about how wonderful the country in which they live, Mermaid start laughing convulsively.

- What do you do, your mother? - angried Babashbek Zholborsmazarov. - How can you laugh in such a situation? You see, what respectable people gathered here?

But Mermaid could not stop at once, it was not laughing already but convulsions, even though she tried as soon as possible to calm a nervous laugh and spasms. Babashbek was deeply shocked by such behaviour of his beautiful wife, she seem to him looking not only foolish, but boorish and uncivilized myrkians woman, and he hit her on the cheek.

Mermaid stopped laughing, her eyes flowed with tears, and she said to her husband:

- Here you are raised for the first time to me yours hand, without any good reason. And if you want to know the reason for my laugh, I tell you, that was not necessary to start the fight against excesses, if all end with the same.

Babashbek Zholborsmazarov frightened by these words of his wife, because loved her much, even if he was a fooish chap. He immediately apologized and promised that would never hit her more. Moreover, he prepared a draft of decree to Parliament that firmly prohibit such sort of domestic violence as beating woman and children in kingdom of Chigu, well informed that similar law long time ago worked in Atlantis.

After that Babashbek tried not shown on public with his wife. But it is difficult to predict and anticipate what await us in close and far future ahead. Despite for the great wealth of the country, many citizens suffered from poverty. And no wonder because ancient Kyrgyz were incredibly idle and spendthrift nation. Wealth that came to him, quickly moving away, because they are used to planning and spending lot of money and resources and time for endless holidays, anniversaries, toys and various pre and post funeral procedures. It was just a such sort of ancient people who wrecked down and maddening from surplus spendrifts and love for fests, leisure and postmortem procedures, ceremonials and days of remembrances.

And need to say that all this happened together with worsening the global climate and world political tendencies and decreasing environment, when often happened droughts, landslides, earthquakes and other calamities and envious and powerful king of the Northern Empire long time prepared to seizure of land of Kyrgyz, even though he have more than enough lands and resourses in own great kingdom, nevertheless he lying eyes on this beautiful country, has seen clearly how naive and non-pragmatic and simple were been their inhabitants and how stupid and weak and irresponsible was been his government.

So that king is going actively to bribing deputies and government officials, and begin gradually to buy up strategic resources of this country. Thus, the country starting to sell at first plants and factories, then energoresurses, then mountain streams, pastures, roads, forests, arable land.

In the end the members of Parliament raised the question about sale of crown jowl of Kyrgyz land the magestic Issyk-Kul, for the paying all debts and credits, which they grabbed from the banks and other financial institutions functioning under the control of northern powerful emperor.

Deputies began to spend one campaign after another to prove simple chigu people that only passing Issyk-Kul as the property to another more powerful and wealthy state would be to help for our small country support its own truly independence. Certainly that was absolutely stupid and dangerous idea but government body and member of parliaments of Kyrgyz ancient state trying to believe for that, making money from such politics and tended to all country believed for and Babashbek also actively invovled to that deal and given the lot of press-conferences about great values of friendship and good relation with the north empire.

Certainly the many citizens of ancient Kyrgyz land disliked such ideas, especially when Babashbek as the native man from Yssyk-Kul valley openly trough leading TV channel and newspapers announced that if we presented our lake to North Empire its not mean that we are left our freedom and independence.

Once after that Mermaid with Babashbek made visit to another party where joined close relates and family friends and conversation turned to politics, God damn it.

It need to say that there was a curious young man who asked the opinion of the Mermaids, regarding the sale of the Issyk-Kul - and whether it will strengthen the independence of the country?

Since Mermaid, as you recall, was the king's daughter, she could not lie, and said plainly that such a step, on the contrary, lead the country for lose independence. This comment has got to media and caused a scandal in society. It turned out the rumor that one of the influential member of Kyrgyz Parliament and his wife contradicted on such important matter.

Babashbek enraged and terrified from such public interview of Mermaid, because he feared that the king of Chigu together with emperor of north great federation will informed about such event and it might case bad effect for his status so when he come at home completely lost temper and struck wife on the cheek. Certainly he forgot at all who is the father of his wife, as the typical Kyrgyz politic, which didn't undestand that resentment and anger of Kol Buudan ata could have far more disastrous consequences for him and his country than displeasure of powerful northern emperor.

- Here you hit me for the second time, instead of being grateful, - said wife. This time she didn't drop from eyes any tears. – Remember, if you again lift up hands on me, you lose me forever. As for the sale of Issyk-Kul, never do this if you not want to lose the country and rise up the hate of father of world water.

Babashbek Zholborsmazarov quickly came to his senses, and fell on his knees in front of his wife and begged her forgiveness, promising that never ever to raise hand on her again

Trying not to tempt fate any more Babashbek decide leave membership in parliament of Chigu, get away from politic and return again to country hoping to live there with wife, whom he loved with all his heart of half-savage Kyrgyz and Aryan.

However, he did not do it in time. One day on the shore of Issyk-Kul gathered the next summit of the countries of vast region of central part of Eurasia who chosen the purely asian path of development and political system. When the kings and presidents once elected to his post or themselves appointed to that by war and revolution, remained there until his death or until the next revolution and mass revolt will swept them from their high positions. Alas, the king of Kyrgyz also trapped by the wrong tradition of cleptocratic rulers and under strong pressure of north emperor began to degrade the course going to freedom, justice and forced moving all country toward wrong ideology and irresponsible and lawless way of governing, pressed out the institution and systems protecting human values and rights of every citizen and states interests as whole from the bad rulers, although it fundamentally contrary to the principles of the Aryan civilization.

In general, such kind political event lasted three days. Head of the region for three days discussing how to organize the Customs Union, and the emperor of Northern powers are arranged so that the Customs Union allegedly promoted the independence of each of its member countries and the rise of its economy. In fact it was clear, that the idea of creating such Union could not bring anything good in principle.

However, Babashbek as friend of king of small country had to play the role of gracious host.

And at the end of the summit was the cultural part, where staggered the play of an ancient kyrgyz playwright, which has been recognized as the model of patriotism's expression.

In the play, a major role was played by famous actress of the country Kyrgyz, the performance was dedicated to the 20th anniversary of the independence of the country. But still - and director and the actress does not love a free country Kyrgyz and Karakhanid USSR, and did not hide their preferences, they believed that until we again do not restore the vast empire, there could not speak about achieving the true independence.

Actress Amal Deydikmatova in the climax presentation exclaimed, "What country we were fucked off" uttering these words in the language of the northern empire that there appreciated how she loved and committed to the revival of the new updated Karahanid USSR

At this very moment Mermaid began to laugh, right in the theater, where she sat with her husband and other politicians, member of parliament and presidents.

- What is this? - outraged Babashbek. - You should be ashamed, to behave in a savage in such a society. And hit her in the face.

At the same moment Mermaid stopped laughing and said to her husband:

- Here you hit me for the third time, without any reason, instead of reward me for what I said. Because I'm not guilty. You lost me forever now. And if you want to know the reason for my laughter, I tell you. Only a free man can appreciate freedom. These actors, directors of theatry and playwriter and author all thought about quite other things, they are not interested in freedom but desire to return to slavery, they were put to them with all heart. That's what I was laughing so bitter in the day dedicated to the anniversary of freedom of your people.

Well, now let's go to the lake, it's time for parting. I leave you, but you will remain with our children, take care of them, and they will take care of you later.

That's how they came back to the shore of the lake. Certainly Babashbek asked and begged his wife many times not leave him, hold her hand, fell to his knees in front of her, assuring her that he loved her too much, and that never-never hurt her, but all was worthless.

Approaching the shore of lake Mermaid shouted:

- Come on, my good cows, sheep, horses! It's time to go home! Come on, let's go, let's go! Kai Gut! Kai Gut! Kai Gut!

The great number of cows, sheep, horses respond to this calling are going down from the pastures to the shore of the lake. If previously there were only 20 sheep, 30 cows, 40 horses, now their quantity grown tenfold.

When Mermaid went to the lake, all these animals followed her and one by one disappeared in the depths of the Yssyk-Kul.

Babashbek stayed on the beach, poured a bitter tears. But his cattle, herd and shoal also multiplied for past years, living with a livestock of Mermaid, his sheep, mares and cows inbreeded with the best animals that gone out of water and became numerous and pedigreed. In general, the number of animals went into the water, as much as remained on the bank - owned by Babashbek. He must no complain for that account, having such wealth. And what's more he had the children – free sons, who grew up smart and responsive and deeply devoted to father. They took care of him, deeply shared his grief. All of them successfully married, bring to house very good daughters in love, one smarter than the other, that also multiplied the joy and happiness of Babashbek.

However Babashbek could not to console himself at all, his grief only increased in short, middle and long term. He nothing to do with.

One day he went to the shore of the lake, and since then no one seen him more. People told that he gone after his beloved, threw himself into the lake.

It is also said that famous earthquake that took place 3000 years in the Issyk-Kul basin occurred precisely because of the wrath of the king of the ocean Kol Buudan-Ata, resulting in a huge chunk of rock collapsed and blocked the Boom gorge, and water flooded most of the Issyk-Kul and many villages and cities of the ancient Chigu disappeared forever under water.

We do not know exactly what was in reality, but the fact remains, the powerful state of the Aryans has ceased existence, people, survivors from that disaster were scattered all over the world, except inhabitants of mountain area, who continue to live this day, as they forefathers but not in ancient quality and tradition when their great ancestors equaled their country to Atlantis.

One day from the "bright future" in the Hell

An extract from ecological tragedy "The golden trap of Kumtor"

http://www.epubbud.com/book.php?g=RRQZG22F
(Kyrgys version)

http://www.epubbud.com/book.php?g=LYJ39VVE
(Russian version)

The full English version displayed late

3 act

(A beach of tailing dam on the site of Kumtor, the great lake where accumulated over 60 million cubes of highly toxic liquid - waste of golden producing mine and plant for the nearly 20 years of activity. For that time also produced nearly 600 tons of gold, 80% of them stolen by the Kyrgyz highest officials and their international "partners" and greedy hunters for the hot money.

The free presidents of independent Kyrgyzstan - Akayev, Bakiyev and Atambayev completely naked with the burnt bodies took the hellish swimming procedures in the cold and acid water. Among them also floundered Levitin, Birshtein, Gurevich, Maxim,

Aydar and many other well-known figures, experts, advisors, the authoritative elders, who supported and covered the treads and schemes of this greatest international golden trickery – they are all now took awful swimming procedures, wallowing, trembling and convulsing in sulfuric acid, experiencing incredible pains and torments.

On the edge of lake, you have seen the central figure of the drama - a great Dragon with the streched wings, that carefully watched as people took bathe in the contaminated lake, and when one of swimmers trying to get to the shore, a terrible monster spewing from the mouth of a long stream of fire, driving the unhappy martyr back to the poisonous and terribly cold water).

Journalist: Oh, Gosh, what's the hellish vision?! Is that a bad dream or it happen in reality? How might be such awful picture?

Dragon: Hey, scribbler! This is not a dream, believe me! Ask those who taken sulfur baths - they will tell you about their harsh realm?

Journalist: Incredible! Our presidents and high officials and their close ones all together swimming in deadly cold and deadly poisoned water? And who were there - far away on opposite side of lake? It seems lot of people there?

Dragon: Yes, very lot. They are all the shareholders of "Kumtor golden mine" who gained incredible wealth - Kyrgyz and their foreign counterparts. Millionaires and billionaires, heads of states, members, congressmen and other rogues and hunters for power and gold.

Journalist: For what injustice they are all so severely condemned?

Dragon: All those who somehow enriched in gold or earned in that matters the political dividends. There are also brokers from international stock exchanges and presidents of companies and intermediaries - all now have wallowed in acid and suffered. The Kumtor mine as you know involved nearly 5,000 shareholders worldwide,

Journalist: Are they all here?

Dragon: Most of them. Those who shown especially hot greediness have taken very cooling baths there, and those who have been less delinquent for corruption or mistakenly involved, they now working at the Kumtor mine with the rehabilitation team. Repaired what they destroyed unwillingly.

Time will come when you too will wallow and swallow acid in the pool if you do not stop to hide the truth and deal with embellishment lies!

Dragon (turned to floating men in the cold water, to those unhappy high officials and VIP persons of Kyrgyzstan, Canada, Russia and others countries):
Come on, tell me, boys, seduced by gold, do that really or not the suffers that you are experiencing here?

(From the mouth of the dragon issued the jet of fire pointed toward the presidents, and heads of all swimmers in great horror disappeared under the water hiding from fire in a toxic solution.

When fire and cloud exhausted and dissipated above the surface of lake first from the water appeared the bald head of Askar Akaev, the first president of Kyrgyzstan, surprisingly close to the shore, where stood Journalist, watching in horror for such spectacular and horrified show).

Askar Akaev: Hey, respected contemporaries, it was not a dream - everything that you see. What I thought before as reality turned out here to the sweet dream and what I could not imagined appears as reality now. How did I could be so deceived!? I beg you, come closer.

(Journalist comes close to the shore of the tailings dam).

Askar Akaev: I know you well. As you to me. After all, you studied at the Polytechnic, where I successfully worked once. I should have to stay there as physicist and not to meddle in politics at all. I was a good scientist... But now it's all gone to past and nothing to do with them...

Journalist: Askar Akaevich, when you came to power, many believed you, thought you were worthy for the highest post. Why we all deceived by you?

Dragon: What do you answer for that, a man worthy to be president?

Askar Akaev: If say honestly I was not worthy to be a president. I found myself in this position accidently as a result of intrigues and dirty political games against my predecessor Masalievs. All his haters and opponents had been ready pay all costs for getting rid of him. As a result I came to power.

Journalist: But even seeing how unfair you came to power, many put up with it, hoping that you will be better Masaliev. And it seems at first you justify these expectations, when you declared course toward democracy. But why you have not established of stable society in Kyrgyzstan as promised many times? You have been really educated and smart man for doing that, so why you didn't do that?

Askar Akaev: You said that - o, my cursed soul! I had everything for the transforming Kyrgyzstan from poverty post-soviet country to the second Switzerland - the knowledge and power, and international support. I have not only one small thing! Love for the Kyrgyz people and correspondingly have not the high moral qualities of truly leader, spiritual and historical grandeurs so typical for the great lieders. I was a good man and not so bad physicist, but presidency transformed me into a petty and vindictive person, who did not see anything, except money, gold, who looking just for strengthening personal power at any cost, who did not know how to defend the national interests of Kyrgyz Republic, who gradually becoming to a jester and clown and zaniness at international area, enslaved by the leaders of great powers. Yes I was their puppet, crouching and trembling in front of them and at the same time condemning own people for stagnation and total poverty. I was not the president at my origin and core, as a result I became a traitor of Kyrgyz people and even after people got rid of me, taking refuge in Moscow, I continued to hurt my people and country actively cooperating with the leaders and politicians who hated freedom and Kyrgyz statehood.

Now I have to you one request, please come close to me.

(Close to the place where stayed Journalists swam up the next also unhappy presidents of Kyrgyzstan Kurmanbek Bakiev and Almaz Atambaev, competing with each other).

Kurmanbek Bakiev: I also have to say something, Zamir. Help me, dear, do not deny me. After all, we are with you from one region, we are both southerners. After all you believed me and one time helped me to become president?

Journalist: Yes, I believed, like most of the people, when you became president, when people ousted Akaev disgracely, everyone believed, including you, that at this time in Kyrgyzstan established equity power and justice. Why that did not happen and we were all failed again after great revolution?

Bakiev: Alas, comrade journalist, politic is a very complicated thing... I really wanted to work for the good of the people, and planned seriously as promised to press out a corruption and family way of ruling. But we all live within the CIS countries, where ventured the similar processes and go out from this circumstance is very difficult. All these countries in one way or other keep up authoritarianism and as we called "family rule" or group, clan ruling forms of government, all suffered from the same systemic corruption and moral degradation of power, society, courts and others. How I could alone did something to correct the fatal mode of government in the country, and even more laying the foundations and firmament of truly democracy? Yes, I have chance for that but did not have the appropriate knowledge, practice and correspondingly the great courage. After all, I was in my previous days just the head of the small industrial plant, the director of strictly guarded

Soviet enterprise and therefore the position of president of free and independent Kyrgyzstan, and even more of the mission of reformator and creator of free economy and society was totally unacceptable to me.

(In that moment Almaz Atambaev extended ahead pressed aside his predecessor).

Almaz Atambayev: Listen to me also, Zamir. After all, we have been together for many years in opposition to the Akaev regime, your newspaper at one time even finding refuge in the Forum, a building that belonged to me. I have always appreciated you as a journalist.

Bakiev: Give me the opportunity and tell what I want to the end!

Akaev: I am also do not say to the end!

Akaeva: Listen to me, too! After all, your ancestors were from Talas, and you are from the same tribe kuchshu which I belonged for. So not give up your relate and listen what we say.

(At this point, Dragon again blew a terrible fire in the direction of the presidents and their wives, and all swimmers quickly hid the head in cold water. Since Journalists stayed close to them, the fire also slightly burned his arm).

Dragon: Now put his burned hand in the water of the tailings, and you will have an idea of the pain experienced by these unhappy persons!

(The heads of presidents again began to appear above the water, one by one).

Dragon (to presidents): Speak one by one, showing respect for each other, unhappy creatures lured by gold and imitating democracy and dragon too and yours greedy wives, that ready go to hell for the sake of wealth and power!

Akaev (to dragon): Very good, sir dragon! (to Journalist) All that you see here, comrade journalist, you must to honestly tell people how it was, when you get back.

Bakiev: Yes, tell about everything, what happened with me, not hiding anything.

Atambaev: Hone his pen better and outline all you have seen here on newspaper, as you can do that when you want it very much.

Akaev: It would be better, if you meet with us and tell all privately face to face.

Journalist: How it possible? Where and with whom?

Akaev: When you return in reality, fly directly to Moscow and turn to Askar Akayev personally. Tell me everything what's going here. Let him not hope to find protection in Moscow, for Putin power and as fast as possible let starting return one by one all the money, assets and gold stolen from the people.

Journalist: You believe that he listened to me, if I said about you swimming here?

Akaev: Yes, believed and listened all you speak to him if you just tell him the truth.

(Three presidents in one time):

Tell them! Tell! Tell!
If you do not tell them, then you will stay here with us forever!
Tell! Tell! Tell them!

Akaev: Tell to him, I mean to me there - let return all the stolen money and assets back to Kyrgyzstan - all that's left him and hidden must have been given to people and state - and tell him also after such restitution let he sincerely repenting and bitterly crying on the face of people, maybe then his suffering here is alleviated

Bakiev: Yes, dear, after Moscow immediately go up to Minsk and meet me. Tell me that fleeing from Kyrgyzstan and hiding in the woods of Lukashenko, hunting there for boars, having no way to see the dear Maksim that is still not a hell. Hell, my dear, here – in Kumtor tailing! Let he return all the money he grabbed and took with him or hiding somewhere around the world, let them return to their homeland and let return himself to Kyrgyzstan and being judged harshly there! Drink vodka in Belarus and complain for destiny, it is not a good. Uh. Zamir, dear, the end of the world and Judgment Day is mot the writing nonsense and fabrications?! How tired deadly my soul from torment and anguish here!

(Atambaev again swam ahead)

Atambaev: Well, they are far away from you and Kyrgyzstan, and I live in the same city with you, Zamir. Tomorrow, without delay, go unto me to the residence, be patient and stubborn but reach me, and tell to president of Kyrgyzstan all about happening here, not hiding a single details, and he'll believe you and maybe change himself and deadly course of country.

Go faster by any means. Bring a meeting with him, find a way for that. Tell me, tell to Farid, my wife, advisors, family and friends about what is happening with me on this side. Let them as soon as possible return to country and people all money and richness and resources stolen from them. Let they not persist with the problem of Kumtor, give it full control of the public and the Kyrgyz government. If you cannot persuade him, I have to tell you, you will also be here and frying in cyanide!

Journalist: Dear presidents, I promise to do everything in my power to meet you and tell you the whole truth about what I see here. But there I going from here, no one will listen me.

Prezidents: Will listen you if you tell whatever you had seen here!?

Bakiev: If you lose all hope and president not believe you - tell him that you have seen on his body a mole.

(After this words Bakiev turned body in the water and twisted his arm back showing a birthmark on his back, under the left shoulders blade).

If you tell him about it, he'll believe you, and accept all what you have said seriously.

Akaev: Very good! I also have a birthmark, which is known only the people close to me. But its place just below.Look!

(Akayev's dived in the water as dolphin, and pop out on the surface for the instant naked buttress, two round hemispheres and somewhere between them placed a brown birthmark and while the head of first president had been under water, he pointed with the finger of right hand to the bithmork, then his body again swerved in the water and the next moment his head appeared above the water again).

Did you see it? If you tell him about the mole and accurately indicate his location, he will ask you, how do you know about it, and you say him all about happening here with him and he believed to you.

Atambaev: Look on my feet also, Zamir.

(Raises his right leg above the water}.

Do you notice a mole? Tell him about it and he'll believe your words and will no longer be in doubt.

(In that time to the discussion interfered the wives of presidents

Wives of the presidents: Look closely and attentively for our bodies, brother journalist. Fix hardly in your memory all their features and geography and intimacy).

The first-ladies dance in mountain lake

(They are swerving on the extremely coldest and poisoned waters
Showing various ultimate places of theirs bodies to me,
One of them pointing on the brown mole on the interim part of thigh,
Graciously shifted it under surface
Other turned back where under the neck
You could observe the large birth mark,
Third trying opens to me the left breast,
Got up it under water
And toss with fingers slightly brown teat
Showing underneath the trace of long age's surgery.
And around the first ladie and ex-first-ladies majestic round
Circling the great quantity of wives of other innumerous top governors -
Prime-ministers, advisers, legislators, Court members -
All of them who were been mixed and participated in Kumtor adventures
For stealing or helped to steal hundredth ton gold
And destroying Kyrgyz ecology
Now swimming in dreadfull tailing Dam
With their dears wives
With fat, average, strong and fragile complexity
Nice, beautiful, gallant, ugly and monstrous
Very diligently synchoswimming
Performing theirs exclusively features and secrets of their bodies
as if I might to fix in my memory all these bodies revelations
for reaching theirs sacred believes.
"Do you see how much we are suffered there? -
cried to me the nicest from them

the prime ballerina of water dance,
Please help us, give us some chance
that you stopping our deathly shameful curse of living
Poisoned with corruption, lies and eternal cursed greediness.
Our men did not to save us?
Please save us? Reach us! Find us!
Might us to believe that happened once
After years of wrong ruling
And destruction nation, ecology and hope for future
For the sake of luck to possess Eldorado).

Presidents: Please be merciful and show pity at least to our wives, if you do not worrying about us. Hope you understand now how hardly we and our wives suffered here?

Journalist: But I told you and warned many times, trying not to conceal the truth that your future could be terrible. You didn't believe me. Well, I'll try to get you again, but I doubt you'll believe me this time too. And your advisers and supporters not let me do it – reach to you they are carefully guarded all gates and ways.

Presidents: Whom about you said?

Journalist: About your advisors, who surrounded you, they will not allow you to know the truth - and rather accuse and condemned as abnormal one, driven into a psychiatric hospital.

Presidents: Adjure you, do not afraid us. From now and onward, we will not pursue against you and yours writing brothers any kind of oppression, not treated secretly you and your family. On the contrary, we will give you the most prestigious job in the presidential administration; will render all possible financial support, as a creative person, sent you as ambassadors to any country where you wish, will present the best apartment in Bishkek. We are very capable and confident about such technologies. Just only one request for you - find way to meet with us, talk and write only truth always. Even if we earlier did not understand and respect you, now the live will go quite differently. We are swear not only you, every honest truth-seekers, human rights activists, who love the justice will support strongly by us. We will know how to do that.

(Akaev, Bakiyev, Atambayev, their wives, advisers, experts began to get out of the water and as the terrible crowd of monsters and vampires starting pursue Journalists, trying to grab him):

If you will not tell the truth, you also died here, so find and convince them to return back stolen money, gold, let they vomit out all that stolen for the country and the people, and let the rest of your life they work hardly for the interests of people and maybe then their suffering will get ease here.

(When a crowd was ready to grab the Journalist, Dragon flashed toward them a jet of fire, stopped crowd and turn it back to the poisonous water – they are all run, spring and dive to the lake saving from fire, but, alas, in the cold water their bodies burn with the acid, that multiplying extremely their sufferings and pains. And addition to in the lake have swimming the big two and free-headed mutant fishes with huge sharp teeth and greedily that fastly attacked sinners of Kumtor, tearing their bodies and dragged into the depths of the pool).

Journalist: Who is that - the sitting naked man under your feet with the face looking to ground? He looked as the glued to ground.

Dragon: Because his eggs stacked with the nail to the concrete margin of basin. This is the national lieder, who trying to catch all the world for their eggs, now himself caught and nailed and enjoying much with that delicate procedure.

Journalist: O God!

(In that moment at the great distance on the sky has shown the airplane flying somewhere.

Dragon waited when airplane flew close and then spitting toward heaven the high energetic burning substance, that rocketed right to the airplane as a surface-to-air missile. After 10 second the airplane was been exploded and destroyed in air and all their remnants with the unhappy passengers fall down to the poisoned lake).

Journalist: Who, what they are! Does it really the MH-17?

Dragon: Yes, sure. It was the same flight and plane just only the equipage and passengers are different.

Journalist: Who are they! The great number of people falling to poisoned water.

Dragon: The deputy of Russian Duma who voted for the war in Ukraine and also among them the lieders of terrorist group, green men and others scoundrels, provocateurs and war wishers between two brotherly nations and countries.

(The deputy from both comities of Russian Duma are faling to the poisoned lake like the autumn apples. Among them clearly have seen the terrorist from Donbass and Crimea with the Calashnikov on hands.

Then Dragon turn to the man with the nailed testucules to the cemented ground and sarcastically asked):

Dragon: Hi! How are you, mister national lieder? You preferred hold forever the strong power and authoritarian rule and do what you want to do as the dictators? I understand and quite agree with you. I am also like unlimited power and when you may all nation catch for their most weak and fragile and painful place and do with them what you want. How nice and excellent procedure for the holder and how utterly bad for whom who caught by eggs!?

(Man with the nailed testiculos to the ground trying to say something, maybe plagued Dragon to kill him and stopped his shame and pain.

Then he turned to Journalist and it would possible to read on the suffered face of teflon president and national lieder of Russia the same asking and implore):

National lieder: Please find me, reach at me. Explain all that you have seen here. And I promised you, that I give you all what you want. You will be the richest man in the world with the dozen billions in the Swiss banks or you preferred to be the president of Kyrgyzstan? I swear, I appointed you dismissed himself Atambaev and never intervened in you politic, not bribed you elitas, planed various plots, downgrade and degrade you lieders, democracy, mood you people against West and

USA under the heavy propaganda from Kremlin. I would only serve for you when you asked me. Yes, I will be president of Russia but worked for Kyrgyzstan. I know what about you thought? I swear that really helped to sustain and support the Kyrgys independence, never more pressed and killed the Freedom and Justice.

(Dragon caught him with mouth, torn out from the ground and tossed this superman-president to the lake).

Dragon: Go to his company and partners and loveliest friends, ideologist and supporters and cherishers.

(Then turn to Journalist):

Dragon: Did you look all and understand? You also will come here, if you will not be honest and not tell what about you have seen here. Maybe you would outskined there if you do properly you duty, job and mission and suffered at mundane but it would be much better for you, than have been out skinned here and take bath in this poisoned water forever. Go away to his harsh reality and try to not meet with me again.

http://www.casestore.co.uk/detail/148282356X/
eleanor-rigby-the-chronicles-of-great-love-and-fall-of-great-empire

http://www.greenmetropolis.com/search.
aspx?results=0&title=Eleanor%20Rigby

The Ping-Pongs ball of great nations

or True history of April revolution in Kyrgyzstan
(tragedy)
Participants:
Concubine President
Deputy of Parliament
Journalist
Historical writer
Religious leader
The spirit of Shakespeare

Act I

Scene1

Outside of small town among the forest near to Moscow.

Old woman with a stick on hand step out to stage, looking carefully down. From opposite side showed Journalist, just walking on fresh air.

Journalist: Good day, grandma!

Old woman: Good day, son!

Journalist: May I ask you, grandma, what you searching for - mushrooms or maybe some berries?

Old woman: What is catch to my old eyes, son. I am getting look for early wild strawberry and gooseberry, mushrooms will be ready in the second part of summer. But this summer promised to be a bad to us.

Journalist: Why you said so, grandma?

Old woman: The weather is especially hot and dry. A summer just starting, and grass and trees suffered from lack of rain and water. Spring was rainless and our summer has no obligates nor resources for compensate the loss of water.

Journalist: That is general tendency, grandma. As scientists from West and others advanced nations emphasized and predicted this is the result of Global warming.

Old woman: Well, it is simple for rich and prosperous people to live in comfort and protection and looking time by time through screen of TV and PC for the Global whether's twist and show. Not so well with poor and unhappy ones with them have played that Global changings. Dear son, where you came from? Kazahstan? Alma-Ata?

Journalist: No, grandma. I came from Kyrgyzstan, Bishkek. But it is close to Alma-Ata.

Old woman: I know. You are going through hard curse of life, I mean your country. God bless you, son, and yours people and country. Our government done wrong thing with Kyrgyzstan this year?

Journalist: What you mean?

Old woman: The tragedy and murders on your capital and changing the rule and the course of your country and government had happened by support of Russian president and their advisers. They must not have done such crime and cruelty and intervened such fatally to the other country and its choice. God don't like it and I am afraid our state also suffered from this sinful intruding. Some catastrophe and calamity had born with that event and increasing and growing unavoidable make up and prepare for us by the heaven justice. If we done wrong things with others, especially with them who sincerely believed and loved us as your people and country.

Journalist: From where you know that grandma?

Old woman: I know... I was feeling with my heart what happened in April there, where you lived. And I am afraid now for my people and Russia, for this town, for Moscow and for that forest that wanted water in such hottest summer.

Journalist: May I ask you another question?

Old woman: Yes, son.

Journalist: You are foreteller?

Old woman: Not at all.

Journalist: And why you know about what happened so far from you?

Old woman: I just believe to God, my son, and afraid that have seen a great lie and evil in some deal of our government.

Many people smart and witty have pretended do not see them or even worse covered a blasphemy and lie with utterly false and misguiding things fashioned as truth. But I cannot to lie and left my family, people, country with a fatal long termed cursing.

Journalist: I work in one of Kyrgyz newspaper, grandma, may I used you words in my article that I planned to publish.

Old woman: Oy! I don't know what to tell you? You want to write what I told about April events in your country...

Journalist: Yes. That is very useful, isn't that.

Old woman: Yes, very well. But, please, not mentioned my name and where I lived correctly and show my picture. I never done such things and don't want to do in my last days. Just say that one honest Russian grandpa who lived somewhere between Moscow and Petersburg didn't received as wise thing what done our government in Kyrgystan and didn't like to tell wrong things and facts for that accounts, because truly believed for God and afraid to do and tell sinful things and asked God forgive us all and be polite and peacefully in future. Shortly say I am desired to all not play with flame and others lives. Never forget to add last sentence!

Journalist: I will do grandma. Hope meeting again in better seasons and fruitful environment and circumstances.

Old woman: God bless you son, be happy and will do ever rightful and wise things.

Scene2

Bishkek. Press-conference the head of country with journalists in his residence. This event dedicates to the honor of victory of April revolution. President, owner of leading newspapers, journalists and expert from various agencies.

President: I am decided meeting with you in that essential historical period for our life and country with aim to inform you what happened really around us - on surface and underneath, - and help you open your eyes, escape from illusions and calling all of us for historic responsibility.

I thought our exiled president Bakiev who run outside cowardly is a bloody traitor and wicked one, the truly political deserter. He had trait Kyrgyz Republic, the hopes of March Revolution and he did the same with Kremlin leader and our strategies partner. As we are all well remembered he many times promised and swore that he go for denunciation of agreement with US about the military airbase, deploying in airport Manas, and not prolong their presence in our land and Kremlin lieder well paying him for that promise but Bakiev changed his decision and broke the promise late after overpaying with other side. Who do such things? Promise to one worlds lieder to be a friend and strategic partner and well paying for that and the same time going to make bargain with other lieder?

We shall not to do the same, we will restoring our good attitude with Russian and I am as a new head of our state promised now that Kyrgyzstan gone for steady denunciation of agreement with US about airbase and doing it in the frame of international law.

Owner of leading newspaper: Do you really planned to outcast the base... in this year?

Journalist (to back side): What's strange announcement pretext the inauguration speech! How rough and crude this post-soviet and post-colonial carelessness, political negligence and childish like nativity, conceit and brutality in one face! Outcast the base... ha. Why no one asked with the same authorities and tone about outcast the Russian military base in our Kant who paying nothing for our budget compare with US troop. But hear first what answered, our dear president.

President: Well... Do you know, have to do it right now impossible. This year I mean. We cannot outbreak the previous signed international agreement according with them US soldiers are staying in our land till the 2014 years. But after that time I swear, the deploying American troop will ended. That's all I say you.

Journalist (back side): Thank for that maestro and master of Revolutions! I afraid that you will do as some of our well payed youngsters and ultrapatriots for money picketing the base and US Embassy with demand "Yankee go home!"

President: We must keep international law but after 2014 years airbase, I promise, left our land forever. That will be I count the honest and right decision that answered for our safety and historical obliges before our strategic ally and closest friend - Russian Federation. I must to say that I have very good and personal warm attitude with president of Russia and proud with it. So we shalll never more to spoil our historical good relations between Kyrgyz and Russian people. As it traitorously done our ranning president.

Journalist: Mister president, you promised one weeks ago in the Ata-Beit cemetery on the meeting in the honor of killed heroes of April revolution, that new forces who came in power will create really honest, transient and responsible system of ruling in Kyrgyzstan, strongly motivated for democracy. You and others member of Interim government showed intention for that. You and your colleagues swore before the buried corpuses of heroes of April revolutions and under the great Kyrgyz national flag that Kyrgyzstan never more returned for the authoritarian, corruptive, one family ruling system of government and produced no more the cursed new theft, traitors, dictators and dragons in power. You have stressed these words and believed them and for our best future, have not you?

President: Yes, I have. We will create the intrinsic parliament system of ruling? And I am strongly believed that our people never will permit anybody in power to usurp our freedoms. Bakiev and Akaev had been our cursed leaders, both of them many told about justice, law and self-government of our people but transformed themselves for corruptive and greedy dragons. We not going with the same road and repeat theirs fatal mistakes more. One of my favorite book, is the play of Mark Zaharov about Dragons. Are you remember the movie made on the base of this play? As a leader of opposition suffered from dragon in power, but after killing dragon, himself transformed to dragon. We made bringing to end this tendencies, I promise you. For that reason we came to power.

Journalist: You are heavily criticized our ex-president. Yes, he was bad politician but the same time you paying respect and showed it for others presidents in post-soviet area. That is look illogically. If you can call Bakiev as dragon and wretch one, what do you thing about other post-soviets presidents? Do they all have the same bad qualities or even much worse than our expelled cursed dragon and what we must done to save themselves from these great associations of dragons, corruptive regimes and empires around us?

President (smiling): I never told such words about others presidents. Honestly say we must have good relation with our neighbors and in the first place for Kyrgyzstan we see Russia. But I am understand you worries so I told rightly to leaders of Russia that we will planned enter to Custom Union and looking themselves and our future with Russian in economic sphere but we will create parliament system of government and keep own way even joining in Custom Union. That is principal question and matter for us. To be with Russian and others post-soviet countries, economically tied with them, but saving own police and intention to create a really parliament democracy.

Journalist (to side): Much better have been to create economic and political ties with congruent powers and countries. In fact we must deserved for harmonious and justice ruling and for better company than that band of post-soviet dogmatics and greedy stealers of common properties. But white a little show respect to aftermath of revolution or bloody plot, hell to know what happened in last April? In any case a curse of our ship changed completely and who might to do any conclusion and prognoses, let look for early step of our new government, before come to conclusion, for our top rulers have seen much better what happened around us and afar. They done it and gain victory.

West has supported us
sincerely and honestly
planting seeds of democracy
and sustainable society
in our crude land,
but hearts of our people
still attached very strong
to old illusions,
and Kremlin genius
very artful and virtuously
played with our post-soviet nostalgias and syndromes,
pushing us back in USSR on and on.

We have hated our freedom, alas,
and greed for instant hot money along.
Humiliation not the word
tell me, experts, how long
this tragicomedy in 1/7 part of world prolong?

Scene3

Meeting of common activists, the members of foundatiuon for supporting Kyrgyz culture, traditions and independence.

Journalist: My friends? Today we are meeting with you to try doing something really valuable for our country. Is it possible or not? Or we are proceeding playing in sand as a little children - as did that our forefathers spelled out by wicked ideology and Russian imperial patronage and authoritarian educations and style of living and governing? Maybe it's time come for stopping reading post-communistic fairy-tales and turn attentions for hard real things and matters?

Historical writer: How strange prologue and provocative discourse in our history! What do you want to say with them? You hurt me with such words – strangely and unfamiliar as if you were been not you. What is happened with you?

Religious leader: Yes, really what about you worries?

Journalist: I met with our president, learn his worries and intentions and have got deeply to conclusion that our new leader is absolutely identical to our previous failed one, whom he expelled and replaced who run shameful away with young wife and grabbed money. I am afraid that both of them keep on the same values and learned the same school of governing and priority and coherent in their depth as political twins? That means power changed again not for the reason of political reform but for the needs and greediness of other staff and elite, just for reshape and gain powers and slightly refreshed rules, concentrating in a new hands, minds and hearts but filled with the same old desires and evil intentions. Such revolution means move to nowhere - nothing change in our government and reality in closed and more far future except things would go only worse and worse. As a next discherished dream and failed hope when one give up and lost spirit. Better not hope at all than failed in hope again and again.

Historical writer: You want to say that Atambaev and his band equal for Bakiev and his supporters? Who expelled own predecessor and heavily criticized them for fatal disease, himself get suffered deadly from the same illness?

Journalist: Yes. And more he wanted to treat the heavy disease, asking helps, supports and advices from the deadly infections friends, the old chaps who born and grown and lived out in USSR where tested, educated and planted the worst kind and traditions of governing. It's look as run to leprosaria for escaping from this fatal decease.

What is that fatal trend? Dream about democracy in tight company with staunch authorities? How you create justice, build its sophisticated and complicated structure from various balances and counterbalances and hoped reach for under the guiding such advisers, holders and benefactors – stealer and killers and haters of really democracy? Better permit wolves to graze sheep and hope for surviving and safety of lasts.

Religious leader: That is a really problem but I know how to help our people?

Journalist: And what you recommend?

Religious leader: Prying to namaz? Go to mosque every day. In one hadis our Allah said bear to me all your worrying. Believe me honestly and I am solved all yours problems.

Journalist: (turn to Historical writer) How about yours opinion? What you suggest for our people for escape from authoritarian net?

Historical writer: Certainly, every our truly writers and journalists and others common leaders must have been patriotically motivated and fight against enemies of our people and republic.

Journalist: So I suggest you, my friends, fighting with our enemies. And select from the list of our enemies the most influential and dangerous of them now. Not in a future or past time but now. I think you agree with me that such calculations and attitude must been most sufficient and fruitful if we are really want to do something valuable for our people - not just tell bla-bla and boasting.

Religious leader: Very well. Our first enemy is our unbelievers, so we must to start praying, right now go to mosque.

Historical writer: Yes, and what else? Let all our people go to mosque every day and create namaz as it really happened in Afganistan and long ago in our region, before the Russian colonization. All our forefathers read namaz, been learned by Koran and nevertheless had not gain any success. Religious is opium for people as said our classic. Only long termed, predominant politic of cruel atheism, practiced by Soviet Union with mass repressions and destroying Islam in Central Asia, help our people make filling better and have really progress in our live. From that point Lenin and Stalin had did a right things for our region - wiping out the religious dominance but badly that it was happened together with terminating all others freedoms.

Religious leader: Please, not tell blasphemy things, my friend. If you want know the communistic ideologies for 90% consisted from Islam.

Journalist: Really!

Religious lieder: Yes, sure. Communist stole the mine principles from holly scriptures and generally did the good things except propaganda of atheism and closing mosque and churches. Therefore the soviet time was a great epoch as one honest attempt to create justice and wise way of governance and life. If only communist lieders made not to despised God their success will gone more great and longer.

Journalist: Very remarkable! It comes up according you who hated and killed us is our best friend, make up the best things for us? I remember in previous meeting you said the same about West culture and Western Europe. You said that Europeans are the same muslims but without Koran and mosque and namaz. Now you say such about communists? How come you got to it and explained such metamorphoses?

Religious leader: That is question of politeness, high culture and education. Whatever help a people to be a happy that might to use.

Journalist: That's OK. We found out the key point of measure. What much helped to us, must been used and certainly protected for using. So without any far and long explain and comment I am ask you, my friends, right now do something really valuable for our dear country and people, whom we are all loved hardly and ready sacrifice our lives for their prosperity.

Historical writer: And what you propose?

Journalist: Protect US airbase in Manas! Write collective letters, appeal for our president, Parliament and who else left in the list of our influential bodies, persons and organizations.

Religious leader: What is the shame! Tush it!

Historical writer: Are you kidding! US airbase no need for protection. These brave soldiers will able destroy our country for one or two hours.

Journalist: But they never do it! And right now they are need for our protection! I explain you why? Look, muslim brother, to me and tell what wrong did you our freedom personally, that you so hated it? What's wrong with you that you completely disorientated? Doesn't that a truth that only after collapse of USSR we gained the real religious freedom and many our people will happy to go to mosque and praying namaz without fear to be a sentenced for their believe?

Religious leader: Yes is that! But... together with freedom our country was been invaded by western religious leader and priest – new Christians, Baptists, Krishnaits and others – that was bad.

Journalist: White a moment, please. You want to freedom but hate it effects and consequences? You must been competitive with own religious believe and do not hate others priests and truth-seekers.

Religious leader: That is a Western propaganda and invention of Sions aksakals.

Historical writer: Yes, we must keeping ourselves from Masons who also don't desire our rise. Yes sure old communists and Russian leaders also do not support our freedom but Western countries also totally governed by Sionists leaders and wealthiest men in world and they trying also to slave us, submit our government and steal our native resources.

Journalist: Ay, my friend, do not poisoned my mind with own arch fears and prejudices. If you believed for protocol of Sion aksakalus and others fairy-tales from secret services that is you right but please keeping our own personal freedom and independence, fighting for that not only for the Islam or against of Israel or West but for our country.

Religious leader: What do you want to say?

Journalist: I mean our real freedom in the Central Asia. Look around and you see everywhere flourishing draconian regimes and dictatorship. Everywhere your colleagues clericals and historians and writer and journalist heavy suffered from lack of freedom. Only Kyrgyzstan able to proud with his freedom, with a small portion of that freedom that existed in Europe. Yes we are still oasis of democracy in Central Asia. And why on Earth we must quenched this source and hope for great region of deserts?

Historian writer: What you mean?

Journalist: Protect airbase of USA and others Western countries in Manas!

West in our hearts

That was the worthiest step and decision
our pressing to US for its airbase in Manas expelling
from our land. The politic so vexed
so self-destructive and depressive
from various points and consequences.

When all our ancestors
from beginning of times, edem and hell
dreamed unlock our region
for west legions,
even if that were a war troops.
We gratefully received Alexander the Great,
for his strong impetus
joining West and East
and after his death
created own legion
of great conquerors,

Act II

Scene 1

Journalist: Who could help me and help to our unhappy country? We are lost, demoralized and beat to death by the enormous witty and cynical enemy, not by the man and one person or group of men and some secret society but by the great country-terrorist, which hundreds years practiced for suppressing and downgrading and wrecking out surrounding nation, states and countries trying broadening it border and make empire. Who we are for that great enemy to able to sustain against? When much a bigger and most advanced nation like Ukraine, Poland, Finn in the West and Japan with China in the East feared the big polar bear? Even the backbone of Europe Germany, the king of sea England and ruler of our world America didn't know how work with Russia. Who we are, our small country Kyrgyzstan in such enormous great scale? It just a fly in international area but nevertheless our country privileged to be an independent state, one of the 2000 member of UN. And we don't waste up this privilege and do all that depend from us to support and save our independence. What would to do in such peculiar historical instants? When all the nation going to hell believing no more to market economy, better future, deeply hurt by very badly setting reform in transition time?

Ode to traitors

You are surrounded us completely
from all sides, covered from top to down
traitors, spyons and enemies of our freedom.

Our neighbors, close relates, friends -
they are all studied in one school and university
where students had prepared, trained and equipped
just for treason of Kyrgyzstan
and do that with high quality and performance.

Yes, my friends, cousins and brothers
we are all nurtured by treason
as our fathers had been traitors
and forefathers also
that lived and survived through treason,
and bequeathed you that as a good tradition
and now you trying be proud and glorifying
and memorizing the treason as heroism.

What is that if not the blasphemy
and treaty and killing the truth
that so hard poisoned our reality
and make way to treason
for the new generation and generation?

How we can stoppage and break
these fabric of replicating endless treasons
have piled layer by layer
in our mentality, history and culture
I don't know, my friends.

Our education, schools, universities.
poitics, traditions, religion,
our past and path to future
densed and based on treason.

We are colonized and prisoned
from all sides
from top to down
by treason and lies.

How we can save
our lands, mountains and pastures
from thousands aggressively and greedy traitors,
totally dominated in our politics
ready sell absolutely all for nothing.

With the red-hot pincers
we must pluck out
all these parasites
from the body of our country
if we want to save our nation.

But I afraid we could not do that
our country and society
so heavily and long suffered

from lack of honest leaders

that maybe our genofonds
destroyed irreparable yet
and passed from not return point
by the long termed practice
slavery, treason and destruction.

No, no I don't believe for such decadence
get out to hell all the traitors of Kyrgyzstan,
I will sing a song this great day and dance.

Journalist is going to sleep in chair.
Room filled with semidarkness.
Entered the man in old English wearing.

Shakespeare: Those should not to sleep a long who planned such
    great thing as you!

Journalist (arising from chair): Who are you and what you doing here?

Shakespeare: You call me and I came to him. I am Shakespeare!

Journalist: Is that possible! How fine! I am so glad!

Shakespeare: Please be patient and left all emotion for theatre. Lets
    look prudently how I can to help you in your trouble which look
    very heavy.

Journalist: How fine! One of the brilliant mind in history of
    mankind come to me and wanted to help me. What else I must
    desire, deserve and hope for? And from the other hand when

such great master played in our side, we must perceived firmly that we are won.

Shaks: Please, not go so fast. We know nothing about nature of success. What I had done in my life was the result of hard work in the specific busunes in the time of revolution. When opened a new windows of opportunities and I used one of them. I am just created the great tragedy and dramas when people suddenly awoken to them.

Are you really wanted to write the great tragic story?

Journalist: Yes, sure, I had such dream. Our state rapidly moving to stagnation and gloomy poverty. hopeless and helpless. And what would do the best in such occasion? Only create the honest story about out new failure and let our future generation would be more happy and lucky and will not repeat our mistakes.

Shaks: I help you, my son, and must say you time blessed you for that.

Journalist: Why, what you say with them? To help me? If you are really want it and did them, it mean decline your Glory, didn't you? If I write really the best tragedy? I honestly tell you envied you and wanted strongly doing something equal, comparing with your genius. If I did it how about you my teacher?

Shaks: I understand you, my son, and not to judge you. In my time I were also to plane overcome the great Greece and Roman writers and playmakers and you could see what happened from that. My name transformed to the Glory of England culture and literary. But do you think that my predecessors Aristofan,

Sophocles and others suffered from my Glory? Not at all! And Dante only add with own Glory to Glory of his teacher Vergilius. Honestly say sometimes I am himself envied for Glory of four boys from Liverpool as you.

Journalist: Really?

Shaks: Yes, after four centuries some my plays lost their fashion, and my words art and poetic magic can not competitive with that music. I say you secretly, you are absolutely right counting their leader as one the messenger of God in XX century. The many their songs inspired by heaven and certainly he have many supporters there too as have in Earth. But returning to our business. So every teacher dreamed about own child and student, because want to conjugate own Glory with posterities lucks

But you case exceptional, I must say

Journalist: What you mean, teacher?

Shaks: Do you know that you are really my son?

Journalist: How might been that?

Shaks: Do you remember the names of your seven forefathers?

Journalist: Yes, I know as every Kyrgyz.

Shaks: Well, and how about you poetic knowledge? You still keep in mind the poem of the greatest Kyrgyz bard about seven seasons of human life?

Journalist: The poem of Jenijok, who born in middle of XIX centure lived 150 hundred years ago.

Shaks: Yes I'd like it very much too, I am who lived 400 years before you and 300 year before Eato. We are both heard this poem from our forefathers and created own versions. This poems mine and Eatos had rooted to the one ancient Kyrgyz dastan called the same name as "Seven seasons of life"

Journalist: Jenijok heard this dastan from Kyrgyz folklore but how you found the same sources?

Shaks: That is the key question contained the great and sacred secret. When I lived in England between XYI and XVI centuries in the time of revolutions and mass disturbs for that country I didn't believe that my fares forefathers who laved 5 hundred years ago before my birth came to England from East. After my dying in other world I have got perfectly dates and prowess for that account and know that my seventh forefather had been Kyrgyz. But I have not right to open the secrets of the world where I live now and theirs enormous stores of dates, knowledgebase and operating heist capabilities.

You only must now and believe me that you are really my son −even betwixt us dividing seven and seven generations. I could say you very much astonishing things, facts, historical and human tendencies and metamorphoses and discoveries, about that never guess ours philosophe.

Journalist: So if you believe strongly that all world are your close relates that is really true, isn't i?

Shaks: Yes it so! But I came to you with more responsible task, my son. Hear me carefully if you want not only gain the great Glory but also help for you people and country to escape from historical rub, long live poverty and misery. And prepare himself for revenger.

Journalist: Revenger?

Shaks: Yes, revenger. For the awful murders of hundredth people. For the traitorous. cruel, bloody and cynical overplot in modern history that called as April revolution in Kyrgyzstan.

Journalist: O my prophetic soul! How much I thought about it and trying to attracts and honored what happened there.

Shaks: That had been bloody scenarios carefully calculated and carrying out under the guide of expert of overplots. But what looking as super canning and supernatural tricks and wicked plan prepared in you world that look as usual sin and ordinary shame from heavens point of view and disposition. For heaven and for Earth much precious and dear thing, my son, its honesty and high level of intention to reach the tautness and courage on this way. Do you really want to gain the eternal Glory, that even you are your father to envy you? Do you count himself as a honest man able to fight and killed the great lie in our history? Do you really worrying about future the majestic holly Ala-Too?

Journalist: Yes, my lord! I will be happy to do something really useful and great for my countries.

Shaks: So go ahead. Create the great poem about the most cruel and merciless tragedy. Show open so called sophisticated method and technologies of **overplot** and revolt, open wide the eyes of your blind contemporaries, try to change their deep wicked and sinful world and their lieders.

And after all if these efforts have not to reach aims, you will be saved himself in any case even if your contemporaries do not been saved.

Journalist: What I must do, father?

Shaks: Look hear, my dear son, I show you the real picture how it happened and later will be officially explained and transformed for the great revolution.

You know that world, I mean West countries, and independents observers after 7th Aprils dreadful events wanted to help investigate the case and roots of this tragedy but Interim Government didn't support this idea. But what happened really on the central square? Who distributed weapons for peaceful meeting makers and participants? According with official explaining the hundreds and thousands Calashes bring out to the revolt men government itself – the chief of intelligent service send to police heavy burdened lorry with weapon and left them on near to Forum where collected mass.

Others evil fact who add for young demonstrates the special mixture from then they are lost completely mind but will be ready for attacking. So young men with weapon and completely lost their mind got up to meeting. Who did it? That is canning combination playing by great evil intellect? The plan was born in the mind of KGB officer. That had been multiple plan against government of Kyrgyz Republic orchestrated and corrected in the time of realization to hiding any marks leading to Kremlin and showing all as a mass revolution against corruptive and ungratefully ruler of Central Asian republic.

Journalist: What I must do?

Shaks: To create a tragedy about April revolution as you did about March Revolution. Show people real picture of what happened in that tragic day. I will help you. Look, what was happen on eve and before the April revolution. And in the end of this show I will come to you again. Take a good look for what had happened at the highest level of these extremely risky days

Curtain rose

Act III

Scene 1

March 2010 year, Kremlin

President Putin: You have really power to discharge Bakiev?

Atambaev: Believe me, Bladimir Bladimirovich, 99 % of our people hated him. That is need only move on small stone from corner of rotten regime and all structure fell down producing avalanche of destruction.

President Putin: Really? I want believe to you

Atambaev: Do not doubt to me? I have a many supporters in the north region of Kyrgyzstan. Especially around capital.

President Putin: And what about south region? Probably you and your friend gain success on capital and North but what if south region had to rise for civil war?

Atambaev: No, no, no, dear president, that is quite impossible. We have many supporters and holders in south also. I tell you 99 % of our people hated Bakiev. Believe me, Bladimir

Bladimirovich, if you stop support this regime it fell down itself.

President Putin: Well, what we must have planned and entertained else except rising price for oil and gas which exported to Kyrgyzstan?

Atambaev: Do what the Kremlin knows the best and shows limitless skill. Media and technical supports, recommendations and assistances. Russian newspapers and TV programs very influential in our Kyrgyzstan and totally dominated there and trained well. Please, help us with strong informational company against our usurper, let our people know perfectly who our governor, look for the truly image and nature of our president and his greedy family.

President Putin: Well, when you plane to start public action against government?

Atambaev: In the first decade of April.

President Putin: Well, we can help you using our own resources and forces, among them the practiced and best instructors, will send them in our base deployed in Kant, from there they try to help you and provide technical supports and others. But I must say that all our support must been keep in secret.

Atambaev: I promise keep them in secret

President Putin: In addition, you must remembered, that success of such operation depend completely from you and yours friends, from you courage's and decides and inner resources for fighting against regime of Bakiev. OK, my man will touch with you lately in Bishkek and you discusse detail and come for agreement and joined plan. If you really come to power you swear me that Kyrgyzstan to stop play with West and US and turn decidedly for the strategic partnership and integration with Russia? Do you promise me that you will not go out from me and Russia later when world and West to start attract you – with money, future prosperity and democracy and others hellish tempts and things? Swear me that you will never been my traitor.

Atambaev: I swear, Bladimir Bladimirovich.

President Putin: And you will expel US base from Kyrgyzstan! Do you have real intention for that or will be try also to mock and dodge us as you ... forerunner

Atambaev: Yes, that is my mine task, to save our people from American patronage and military presentment in our country. Would I get up to top of rule or not, I leave as honest and intrinsic ally of Russia. That is my principal position and disposition.

President Putin: Bakiev also many promised to us to do that and we well paid him for that but he eventually deceived us. I am hope you will not repeat his fatal mistake?

Atambaev: Don't worry and doubt, Bladimir Bladimirovich.

President Putin: OK I wish you success in yours intentions, what you keep in mind and what the result your will succeed. Good bye.

Atambaev: Good bye, mister President.

Atambaev exit.

Enter expert and Instructor for designing and carrying revolts, plot in various unstable and weak Eastern countries:

President Putin: What do you thing, Trofimych, about our guest from Kirgizia? Do we have really chance for success there?

Expert: I think so, president. The government power is traditionally weak, people dislike and disbelieve for their governors and more this country and nation separated mentally and geographically for two regions and tribal differences also very strong there.

President Putin: How about weapon resources if peaceful demonstrators decided attack the White House?

Expert: In the top government bodies we have loyal for us officials they ready assisted not only the plot of oppositions lieders but we are have own staunch and testifying lings and contacts. So referring for this and others good coincidences and possibilities we must have some hope that opposition leaders might be reach to success if what they said and asseverated us about Kyrgyz peoples totally and predominated hatred to regime of Bakiev are really truth.

President Putin: Yes, let will hope for success. So go immediately to South and work there under my specific and high priority order. If you done all skillfully and smooth, I will granted you with more respected appointment and position. Maybe you dismiss

Rogozin, other our patriot, certainly after dismissing Bakiev and expelling US base from Bishkek.

Expert: Thanks a lot, Bladimir Bladimirovich? But where go Rogozin, if I capture blue bird?

President Putin: That is not your problem, dear, do well and correct what I send you for, be honest, kind and preside with me and my staff and you will not forgotten and will granted by me. Remember, I am always working with men not with system. So I believe and want believe to people not for the systems. System is only fiction, even such strong and great as USSR must one day destroyed but belief, the sense of comradeship and collectively responsibilities for our past and future and what happen now on our eyes around us will never destroyed and vanished. We must reunite the scattered parts of one whole - the great Russian state and preventing all attempt in future to dismantle and diminish our power. And I am rewarded limitless whom who served me and Russia with limitless efforts, diligence and skillfulness.

Expert: Glad and happy to serve you, Bladimir Bladimirovich!

President Putin: Go to deal and hold lings with me.

Expert: You are forgotten, dear president; ask me about by interview with leaders of opposition. I separately met with all of them, who came to Moscow, discussed and exchanged with opinions for various questions.

President: Yep. Sorry. And what you found there?

Expert: The situation is very intriguing.

President Putin (cull to secretary): Anna Ivanovna, I ask you call to other bundle of comrades from Kirgisia for meeting the next day. But tell them that I have not much time for them. Only for 5 minut to everyone and keep our meetings with every one of them from others. Let hear what they said and promised separately as they came Moscow and arranged there hiding from each others and from people? (turn to Expert) Yes, hear your - what kind of persons they are all? Do have really among them similar figures as their leader, who visited me yet and pretended be the next president?

Expert: It's hardly to say now but I am fixed their suggestions and sentences for Moscow there. Let hear their declares that I collected here and saved under the headline as "The carrousel of traitors"

He show compact-disc, entered it in computer.

President: The carrousel of traitors? Hm! They are traitors for whom?

Expert: Certainly not for us.

President: Therefore they're our friends.

Expert: That is OK. Please hear audio clip and look for that little screen.

The both look for the screen of special equipment with size of mobile telephone.

On the wall projected the images of Kyrgyz oppositions leader one by one with short declarations

Expert pressed the baton, clearly heard the cracking sound.

First leader: I promise firmly expel the US airbase, please tell about that the Kremlin head. Long live the savior of Russian people. Not only them but all CIS countries, theirs people so tired from freedom and dermocrasy...
Press baton.

Second leader: I promise strongly that Kyrgyzstan joined to Custom Union... No one other candidate do that so precious and wonderful than I am. Please appoint me for presidency, help to national leader of Eurasian to do right decision, believed me strongly, you don't disheartened from me ever... I present you personally my resorts home on the edge of Ysyk-Kul if Putting selected me for presidency
Press baton.
"That is very tempt full isn't that?' – "Yes, sure"

Third leader: I promise, dear president, that Kyrgyzstan deployed on its land Russian airbases and other militaries bases and troops as much in quantities as you wanted and liked them. If you pleased we were transform our country for one great military air carrier, to one solid steel ship with rocket on their every mountain peck and these colossal vessel start to war swim breaking core the Eurasian continent....Turn to cursed West and America...

Press baton. "What amazing fantasy have had some candidates!"

Forth leader: I swear you, dear president, if you pleased me, I am ready to joined completely Kyrgyzstan for Russia.

Press baton "That is old song, many time heard it"

Fifth leader: If you pleased dear president. You just help me to appointed for presidency of that independent Kyrgyz Republic and I'll totally quitted by that freedom and independence not only joined this land for Russia but also heavily diminished their populations, transformed it through severe outside migration to free land for you service.

Press baton. "That's enough, I thought"

President: Yes, sure. The case is very complicated and looks simple and plain also for truly masters of overplots, isn't it?

Expert: Yes, dear president.

President: But be carefully and precise in yours calculates risks and suggestions. Even for demonstrators with weapons very difficult to go for decided steps and break the resistance of government forces.

Expert: Don't worry, president, for some parts of most decided and raged young men who advanced ahead on first line of mass mowing to White House we planned help with some medicine, add unobservantly to alcohol or tea that made them tenfold brave and courage. After drinking one portion of vodka with such adds man transformed for epic hero for 24 hour, completely lost self-control but must be guided by their leader and ready to sacrifice himself as ideal soldier-robot. Police will beat him but he sensed nothing only strengthening his rage, shot and wounded him but he will go and crawl ahead until killed and quenched at all.

President: Good. But I ask you keep in deep secret our participation. Kyrgyz people as whole in north and south very friendly attitude for us and we must save that sympathy and escape from president who trying run out from our control.

Act 4

Scene 1

Journalist and Shaks

Journalist: O my prophetic soul! O my unhappy country and nation which so densely inhabited by such waste amount of traitors!

Shaks: It's no time for lamentation. Instead we must operate quickly and skillfully. We must change some subconscious tyings, knots and clots into the leader's mind and brain.

Journalist: What?! Do you really believe to Dianetica, Freud and Kashpirovsky? And for the final rehabilitation of cursed mind?

Shaks: Yes, certainly. We are all suffered from lack of knowledge and light. Show me the king, tsar, dictator and tyrant who will want to leave forever as a bad gay. They are all dreamed about immortal glory, victory and love and respect from their latest generation. The problem is in our tempt full and weak attitude toward our powerful contemporaries. We love our wrong governor and made them have done wrong steps. All people around the world thought and acted identically and gone with the same way without any exception.

Journalist: I thought the national lieder – is exceptional case.

Shaks: Not at all. He is a usual citizens of great country, born, educated and grown by Soviet empire. Ready devout his life for the great idea in past but later informed well about fatal ideologyies and turn to restoration of Russian great identity. He is a man flooded by great ideas, mainly by ideas of saving Russian people and greatness from West. Certainly he not a stupid politic and undestand that Russia is a part of Europe and could not survive without West.

Journalist: Of course he understood all but wanted just a little play with West partners for that Asiatic games. What we will do in such non ordinarily case?

Shaks: I'll help you to reach him in dream. You go to him and honestly talk with him about very serious things and matters.

Journalist: What about? And how even in dream equally told with such influential and monumental person like a marble stature, so deathly locked for communication?! And by the way who I am, to learn him and give him advice?!

Shaks: I will send your to Him in early period of his life when he was young boy, comsomolets and you must to find way to help him escape from some illusions about USSR, that he kept in his soul and subconscious from that time. Show him who are really the enemy of Russia and their destroyers. Go, I have get you correct and precise recommendations what to do and how to do. Journalist:

Scene2.

Journalist and Young national lieder.

Journalist: What do you thing if you have been a president of Russia?

Young national leader: Am I?

Journalist: Yes, you are Bovan? Imagin that you are the head of great country right now?
What you do?

Young national leader: I don't know. Never have got such things. It is quite impossible.

Journalist: Yes, but swear me that never will support and attain with theft and stealers and hope for only secret services if you ruled by country. Because I will show your right now what happened with them who forget about plain and simple things, then going to the Olimpus.
Never forget that every our thought and plan blazed in heaven and if you desired prosperity and happiness for Russian

people as I am for Kyrgyz people, please never forget about this simple facts and rules.

Young national leader: I swear. With pioneers honesty! But why you have got me such strangely recommendations?

Journalist: Because heaven blessed you. Namely you for save Russian from very bad and fatal kind of presidency. Right now! You give yours consent? Save you country, boy, come up to the head of great country and lifted (embarked) for shoulders the historical responsibilities for Russia in one of very complicated period of time.

Young national leader: Yes, I am ready!

Journalist: Do you ready fight with cruel enemies of Russia till the last drop of you blood! Repeat if you are ready.

Young national leader: Yes. I am ready and sweared that will fight with cruelest and nastiest enemies of Russia till the last drop of my blood!

Journalist: Well done. Now I show you the most dangerous and cruelest and traitorous enemies of Russia. Go ahead, Vovan.

Young national leader: Where we go?

Journalist: In a future of Russia?

Young national leader: How we can go them? You have got time mashing!

Shaks: Yes, sure. For example I came here from XYII century. But we have got correct and precise shape of future without any time mashing, if we know what about things, hoped for and what afraid the people, the most average and common citizen. That is simple! You are the most average and common soviet boy, the comsomolets with burning heart for the future of USSR isn't it? Who adored the Soviet noble intelligent services, the highest ideals of Marxism and Leninism, who desired to bring eternal happiness, peace and happiness not only for the Russia but for the rest people and nation around Globe and so on.

Young national leader: Yes, sure. But you are not... espionage from West countries? Or **secret** agents from FBI, Mossad and others enemies of USSR?

Journalist: Or not, not, don't worry. We are just plain tourists from a future - I am, and my counterpart from a past. Please if you didn't know - the great playwright in the world sir William Shakespeare.

Young national leader: Really!

Journalist: Look hear for my proof that I came from 2013 years that is equipment called I-phone I am press the baton and you see...here on screen the Moscow in a future, and you might call to everyone and show them and have access for every library, museum in Moscow and round the World.
Young national lieder: How beautiful!

Shaks: And now I show you my proof about me - who am I really? You see that I speak with strong English accent on Russia and also (he entered hand to his breast pocket and have got out the small piece of yellow paper) that is my sonnet number 151. Look for the mild tissue of paper and color and style of typing machine in our time quite different compare with yours printing technologies.

Young national leader: Yes I believe that you are from others times. But what can I help you?

Journalist: Do you really want to help a Russia and USSR?
Yung national leaders: Yes, sure as every honest soviet man.

Journalist: So, go ahead!
Yung national leaders: But meeting with you that is so exceptional case that I must informed about you my older friends.

Journalist: From KGB?
Yung national leaders: Yes sure. I don't want to be a traitor of my great country.

Journalist: And you suggested that we are traitors and enemy of your country?

Young national leader: The question is next - does you visit in our time have some trouble for our country or not? In any case I must inform our elders about you.

Journalist: The question is next - has live in KGB or not? Do we have able to save honest and wisdom like officer belonged that corporation or not?

Shaks: If you inform about us to KGB, we are all have been prisoned. But after two day we will vanished from prison-house - to return safely in our times but you left under the suspicious in prison for long time. So be wise and not spoil attitude with secret and sacred services nor with delegation from... future and past.

Young national leader: I don't now... What we are do and where we go?

Shaks: Go ahead. You have seen the really enemies and friends of Russian and USSR. And after returning from our trip if you pleased to tell his old brothers what you sow and understood.

Journalist: Sit down here the future president of Russian and his savior!

Young national leader: You are joking!

Journalist: Not at all! You have really chance for that! If you every time and everywhere do the best thing, learn well, be polite and skillful and keep own plans, intentions and missions about USSR and Russia. With one word to say if you been as Shtirlits, yours favorite hero, even better than him.

Young national leader: Did Shtirlits been a real great hero, didn't he?! You are doubt that such person really existed in soviet intelligent services.

Journalist: Nor at all. We are wish you only to be better than him.

Shaks: You must been better than him if you really want to save your country. He undermined the fascist Germany but you must delve one yard below your mines, and blow not only outer enemies but also interim.

Young national leader: Who is the our interim enemy?

Shaks: Usually stupednes, foolishness and personal stubbornness in power and greediness weared in cloak of patriotism. When you just want to keep high position and ready to kill not only his son or brothers or father but own dear country also whom you so beloved and adored. That is very strangely indeed when honest man planned to come in power to serve for fatherland and even save them and doing in first year of his services relatively the right things but lately starting love more and more himself in power than dear country and if he strong and inventive and lucked enough, that is must end very tragically for his beloved country. He simple killed his dear country with own death. The country will buried with him as in the ancient time after death of pharaohs their close people also killed and lied with them in one great grave and cemetery.

Young national leader: You I have got intended to say that USSR lieders – Lenin, Stalin. Krushev, Brejnev and their comrades in theirs politics guided with only desire to keep own power and influences.

Journalist: I think so!

Shaks: I am absolutely believed for that. Certainly some of their lieders have a great impression for world, I mean Lenin and theirs almost inhuman- like energy, diligence and decidedness and excellent writing skill and intellectual potency and impertinence in the fight for the sake of proletariats. But he liked break rules and didn't count at all with moral code and principles in politics and life. He sincerely believed as Pitter the Great and Hitler that for the sake and prosperity of people and empire all means and treats are useful even the most cruel and inhuman and barbarous - even if we must go to killing half of that people.

Journalist: So these leaders one by one pressed and killed the country, their energy and human resources long years after October Revolution. No one didn't care of people real happiness as their declared but only for their personal safety, respects and Glory. Certainly such system will be rocked for fall.

Young national leader: You want to say that USSR one day would will dismantled and vanished?

Journalist: I know what I said. USSR dismantled and vanished but Russia left in the end of XIX centure

Young national leader: And what happened in XX century with Russia?

Journalist: They are proceeding the same tragic course, even throw out the communistic ideology and planned to build market economic they are did the same fatal mistakes. New national leader whom Russia firstly believed as for the intrinsic savior of country suffered from the same old decease. Instead of using his great skill and carefully organized net of services and resources leaving from KGB for the benefit of Russia and opened historical possibilities, he starting to restore old and rotten system, creating new post-soviet burocrasy. Instead to learn rude mass and invest money for people and their real education, he invest for new elite, shared with them the national treasure, produced from closest friend the new generations of billionaires who know and tamed nothing more except exploiting mass and living for sales of recourses. He raised fatal corruptive and irresponsible and traitorous generations of new elite.

Shaks: After that great combination with his appointment for the new presidency, time come for others trick. We must extracted from prison the worthiest evil and murder send him for Moscow and gave him real power as we might honest man and most successful businessman to prison for life. You must elected himself again and again for highest post in great country, breaking all rules and Constitutions, manipulating with mass-media and TV show as you want. That is all possible if you real chap with power and atomic bomb in hand and completely slaved population. That is my game, he said. And people don't know how to stop him.

Young national leader: And what you suggest and advise for truly patriot of USSR and Russia?

Journalist: Really have got, doomed himself for saving Russia!

Shaks: Yes, prepare himself for great deed. Not only perfectly learn and study the soviet ideology and science but also the intrinsic history of their progenitors – the rising and fall of

Russian tsarist, Mongolian, Karahanid empires. But much at all learn the secrets and roots of success and strengths and elastic self-repairing powers of Europe and West. Try avoid from strong protection and ban of your staunch communists elders and jealousy orthodoxies, they preferred to build the happy eternal society with completely closed eyes and without any competitions. That is quite impossible to erect new comfortable building without carefully select and prepare good team. Profligacy and negligence only multiplying chaos and hell.

Young national leader: Is it possible to reform USSR and their politic and ideology?

Shaks: Yes, sure as every tyrannical and despotic regime based upon slavery and servitude.

Journalist: We just only guide by truly and healthy friends and ideas and suggestions? If we want create open society and justice government we must going with states and countries have gained success on this way. Not join and flirted with corruptive and evil powers and despotic regimes. Communicate with them and make trade and economic ties if they influential or living as your neighbors but keep strongly and protect your intrinsic own way leading gradually but unavoidable for prosperity and salvation.

Young national leader: And what and where such countries for us? And whose ideology, science and achievement and practice will most preferable for us?

Journalist: Certainly West Europe, US, Japan, South Korea. Every nation and country there created and established real honest and responsible and selected government submitted for law, without frauds and manipulations on Court and election, without theft in powers and games for prudency.

Young national leader: Does communist leaders planed to achive the same aims and results?

Shaks: Yes, they planned so but no one of them had done it in time. Every time they hoped keep for himself some benefits from old system – who wanted to prolong his presidency or stopped little Court or desired some privileges for relate or afraid from worlds authoritarian leaders or rewards from them for clumsily - as a result they drowned personally and had sunken the whole country in new or refreshed and recolored despotia.

Young national leader: Was that a true story of our rise and full?

Shaks: Absolutly.

Journalist: Not only for Soviet and Russian but for all western and eastern, north and south empires and despotism.

Shaks: All the world suffered from the same decease and evilness, called egoism.

Дочь Океана

Согласно археологическим данным, четыре тысячи лет назад озеро Иссык-Куль было значительно меньшим по объему и площади, чем теперь. Древние селения и города, процветавшие когда-то, были затоплены водой после того, как произошло знаменитое землетрясение, описанное в древних источниках, вследствие чего русло вытекающего из озера реки было перекрыто упавшей горой, Боом и Чуй обмелели, а Иссык-Кульская котловина наполнилась водой и приняло тот вид, который знаком нам теперь.

Однако в прошлом все было по-другому, здесь на ныне затопленных обширных землях существовала цивилизация, которая называлась арийской.

История, которая описана нами, произошла именно в эту эпоху, и искушенные читатели сами могут убедиться в том, насколько автор был строг и беспристрастен в описании эпохи, когда по словам древних историков, этот край был одним из центров всего мира.

В один из дней, в те далекие времена, в малолюдной южной части Иссык-Куля, в отдаленном его уголке на берегу пустынного озера пас овец молодой человек, сын одинокой женщины. Их дом и загон был расположен в предгорье, но он пас овец на берегу озера, на холмах, покрытых сочной зеленью, вплотную и круто подступающих к голубой воде.

Так вот это был обычный день, когда пастух ложился на траву и позволял себе забыть о накормленных овцах, которые тоже отдыхали в послеобеденное время и не было никакой опасности, что они могут куда-то запропаститься, потеряться в зарослях облепихи на берегу озера или деваться еще куда-то.

И вот когда он глубоко задумался о том, как прекрасен этот мир и озеро, как он полон всяческих тайн. Неожиданно юноша услышал звонкую девичью песню, которая раздавалась со стороны озера.

"Что это за наваждение?", подумал про себя юноша и, поднявшись с зеленой травы во весь рост, повернулся в сторону Иссык-Куля.

К его изумлению, он увидел девушку, медленно плывущую на мелководье и поющую чудную песню. Казалась, она не обращала никакого внимания и даже не замечала стоящего на берегу юношу, хотя кроме них никого не было в этой части обширного озера. Более того Русалка не переставая петь чудную песню подплыла совсем близко к берегу и забралась на один из скользких, покрытых водорослями больших и плоских камней, коими так изобилует южный берег озера на разных своих глубинах. Она пела, подставляла свое лицо лучам солнца и любовалась собой, глядя на свое отражение в чистой глади воды, поправляя и причесывая длинные золотые волосы пальцами. От дивной песни и голоса девушки казалось даже певчие птицы в зарослях облепихи, барбариса и карагачевой роще на берегу примолкли, зачарованные не менее юноши.

Пастух направился как во сне к кромке воды. Девушка была настолько красивой и необычной, что молодой человек не просто сразу же потерял голову, но и отчаянно стал соображать, как и все обитатели этого края, как бы завоевать это чудо. Он вытащил из своей пастушьей сумки то, что, туда положила мать. Это был свежеиспеченный круглый хлеб и протянул его в сторону девушки.

Но Русалка, когда юноша подступил к ней, соскользнула с камня в воду и отплыла на безопасное расстояние. Затем прервав свою песню, она обратилась к юноше с такими словами:

Тартуулаган токочун, боз жигит,
Отко бир аз катуу какталып,
Жарабайт мага мындай белегиӊ,
Сен дагы мага жакпадыӊ...

После этих странных слов девушка скрылась в глубине вод. Молодой человек остался один на берегу огромного и пустынного озера, при этом его охватила ужасная тоска, ибо он почувствовал, как и все пылкие иссыккульцы, что без этой девушки ему не жить на этом свете.

Он долго стоял на берегу озера в тот день, надеясь что девушка вернется к нему, однако она не вернулась.

Пригнав овец поздно вечером домой и, загнав их в кошары, он тут же все подробно рассказал своей матери о необычайном видении и попросил ее совета – как бы он мог приворожить к себе такую красавицу, чтобы, в конце концов, взять ее в жены.

К слову сказать, его мать была умной женщиной, и отнеслась с глубоким пониманием к его внезапно вспыхнувшим чувствам, сказав ему следующее: "Постарайся не терять голову, сынок. Возможно, разгадка кроется в тех словах, которые она сказал тебе. Так и быть назавтра я спеку тебе токоч на слабом огне, чтобы тесто было мягким, слабо пропеченным, и вот когда ты снова пойдешь пасти овец на берег озера, предложи-ка ей этот хлеб, посмотрим, что она скажет на этот раз? Может, такой хлеб понравиться ей больше?"

На следующий день уже довольно рано, юноша был на берегу озера, при этом он неустанно смотрел в сторону озера и, казалось, почти полностью забыл о пасущихся овцах. Но Русалка не появлялась. Он поднимался на зеленые холмы и снова опускался к воде, Но девушки не было видно. Перед ним простиралась бесконечная тоскливая гладь голубого озера.

И только уже близко к вечеру, когда он уже собирался домой, он в последний раз кинул взор на озеро - и увидел свою знакомую, плывущую у берега.

Юноша поспешил к ней навстречу и, подойдя вплотную к воде, когда между ними оставались какие-то считанные метры, он вытащил из своей сумки токоч и протянул его в сторону девушки, умоляя ее всем видом, чтобы она не уходила от него.

Девушка, заметив его, обратилась к нему с песней:

Белек кылган токочуӊ кам экен,
Сага дагы таӊ болдум,
Зиректигиӊ аз экен,
Сен мага жакпадыӊ, жаш жигит…

После этих слов, Русалка отплыла на глубину и скрылась в воде.

Но на этот раз влюбленный юноша заметил про себя, что девушка улыбнулась ему, прежде чем скрыться в воде.

Это он воспринял как добрый знак для себя, и решил во что бы то ни стало добиваться исполнения своего сокровенного желания. Вернувшись домой, он рассказал все как есть своей матушке, и спросил снова ее совета.

Мать наутро ему спекла медовый токоч, смешав тесто с отборным изюмом и дроблеными зернами ореха, какие обычно пекли в наших краях издревле на праздниках наши родители.

Таким образом, в третий раз юноша пришел на берег озера - на встречу со своей судьбой. Девушки долго не было и на этот раз. До обеда на берегу озера шел дождь, а во второй половине дня погода изменилась, как это часто бывает на Иссык-Куле - и выглянуло солнце, и озеро заиграло всеми красками летнего дня. Но девушки все не было видно.

И только вечером, когда он уже потерял всякое терпение и ему пришли в голову мрачные мысли о том, что ему не жить на этом свете без этой девушки, он услышал снова знакомое пение, доносящее со стороны озера.

Русалка плыла в воде, пела самую чудную в мире песню, и когда она близко подплыла к берегу, юноша протянул ей мягко испеченный матерью праздничный хлеб.

На этот раз девушка не отплыла от него. Джигит подошел вплотную к ней, ступив в прохладную воду, она взяла его подарок, более того они, взявшись за руки, вышли на зеленый берег.

Молодой человек тут же признался девушке, что он жить не может без нее и попросил ей стать его невестой.

Девушка, улыбаясь, слушала слова юноши, а он продолжал и продолжал говорить ей, что без нее его жизнь не имеет никакого смысла, что если она откажется от него, то он тут же бросится в воду - в самом глубокой затон на берегу и покончит с жизнью. В конце концов, Русалка согласилась, но прежде поставила перед ним одно твердое условие.

"Я буду твоей женой, и буду с тобой всегда, верна и предана тебе, буду вместе в счастье и в горе, даже когда тебе и твоему народу будет так тяжело, как не было никогда в прошлом, но помни, что ты потеряешь меня, если трижды поднимешь на меня руки, без всякой на то причины и основания".

Конечно, молодой человек сказал девушке, что это абсолютно невозможно, что он никогда даже не подумает о том, чтобы обидеть ее, что она может не беспокоиться на этот счет совершенно, даже если она провинится, он ни за что не поднимет на нее руки.

После этого они расстались, договорившись встретиться назавтра. Девушка перед тем, как ступить в воду, сняла со своих ног изящные сандалии, расшитые жемчужными крупными бусами, сорвав один из жемчугов и протянула ему, после чего скользнула в воду и исчезла в глубине.

Юноша возвратился в тот день домой, счастливый и переполненный самых светлых надежд, как никогда в своей жизни. Рассказал обо всем, что случилось матери, поблагодарив ее за вкусно испеченный хлеб и показал жемчужную бусинку.

Назавтра он снова придет на берег, при этом празднично одетым, как посоветовала ему мать.

Как и в прошлый раз, он будет долго ждать Русалку. В конце концов, он почувствует себя оскорбленным и даже разгневанным, ведь кыргызы, в особенности иссыккульцы, очень быстро приходят в гнев, он даже подумал, что Русалка всего-навсего лишь пошутила над ним. "Что же, я покажу тебе, - подумал про себя юноша, - какой я шутник". – Он взобрался на высокий холм, который нависал над глубокой водой, чтобы оттуда броситься вниз головой и покончить с жизнью.

И в самый последний момент, он услышал грозный окрик:

- Стой! Ступай назад на берег!

Юноша оглянулся и увидел на берегу озера царского вида величавого старика и с ним рядом стояли три похожие друг на друга красавицы.

Когда джигит подошел к ним, суровый старец обратился к нему со следующими словами:

- Так ты просишь руки моей дочери? И кто же ты такой на деле?
- Я - Бабашбек, - ответил ему юноша, - я родился здесь и вырос. А вы кто такой?
- Я - Көл Буудан ата. Отец всех вод на свете, царь и бог рек, озер, морей и океанов. Если ты будешь достойным моей дочери, я сделаю тебя безгранично счастливым, и ни один царь на свете не сможет покуситься на тебя и твой народ, а если будешь недостойным - я перестану тебе помогать, и ты сам увидишь, что произойдет тогда с тобой и твоим народом.

После этих загадочных слов Көл Буудан ата обернулся к своим дочерям:

- Но прежде ты должен угадать, какая из моих дочерей
  твоя любимая?

Пастух посмотрел внимательно на трех девушек, они были все похожи друг на друга, как близнецы, одеты одинаковы, как принцессы и было совершенно невозможно определить, какая из этих троих красавиц была той самой Русалкой, с которой он говорил вчера. Теряя надежду и уже решив просто наугад выбрать одну из трех красавиц, юноша опустил глаза долу, и неожиданно обратил внимание на то, что на изящных сандалиях на ногах одной из девушек, не хватало жемчужной бусинки. Юноша указал пальцем на эту девушку – и в тот же миг аксакал и двое девушек исчезли из виду, и на берегу озера остались юноша со своей возлюбленной.

- Ну что же, принимай подарки от моего отца, - сказала
  Русалка, - начинай считать как можно дольше на одном
  глубоком вздохе.

Юноша сделал глубокий вздох и принялся считать – раз, два, три, четыре, пять, шесть…

По мере того, как он считал, из воды стали выходить откормленные породистые овцы, один за другим и смешиваться с его пасущимися на берегу овцами. Юноша на одном дыхании смог насчитать до двадцати - и стал богаче на 20 отборных овец. У него самого ыло в отаре около 40 овец, но они не были такими упитанными и породистыми, как те, что вышли из озера. Пастух быстро смекнул, что с такими роскошными овцами, он станет несметно богатым в будущем. Но самое удивительное было еще впереди. Русалка подошла к одной овце и раздвинула пряди шерсти на ее спине, и юноша увидел, что густая шерсть овцы-мериноса содержала в себе золотой песок!

-   В каждой овце в ее густой шерсти ты найдешь много золотого песка, они стряхнут его, когда придут домой, - сказала Русалка. - А теперь сделай глубокий вздох и начинай новый счет!

Юноша снова принялся считать. На этот раз из воды стали появляться породистые отборные коровы, грациозно покачиваясь, одна за другой. Смекнув и слегка поднаторев в этом упражнении, на этот раз юноша смог на одном дыхании насчитать до тридцати - таким образом, став обладателем тридцати великолепных дойных коров.

После того, как юноша немного передохнул, девушка сказала ему опять, чтобы он начал новый счет.

На этот раз из воды стали появляться превосходные аргымаки и скакуны. Юноше удалось довести счет до 40, пока у него совсем не осталось воздуха в легких – он стал богат на 40 лошадей, каждая из которых была настоящим сокровищем.

Таким образом, наш герой не только стал обладателем кызыл жолук, красной косынки, как говорят кыргызы, но и при этом стал очень богатым человеком.

Они возвратились вдвоем к нему в дом и стали жить и поживать счастливо и беззаботно, наслаждаясь всеми прелестями жизни.

Однако это было только начало удивительной карьеры Бабашбека.

Они жили многие годы в горах, счастливо и беззаботно, чтобы он ни делал, он был успешен в делах, у них родились и выросли три сына. Бабашбек стал весьма авторитетными среди своего народа. Но эта была только видимая всем часть благословений. Могучий Океан, Кол Буудан ата, благословил не только молодую семью, но и весь его народ, который проживал в древней Иссык-Кульской котловине. Мир и процветание пришли в эту часть земли. Прекратились не только голод и лишения, но также и войны и нашествия врагов. Все думали, что это просто случайные совпадения, однако в действительности, то было дело рук могучего покровителя вод на земле Кол Буудана ата, который таким образом поддерживал свою дочь и зятя.

Вот так произошли неслыханные вещи в царстве древних кыргызов Чигу в Иссык-Кульской котловине. Страна древних ариев обрела не просто независимость, но и стала весьма влиятельным государством, и на международной арене того времени стали даже поговаривать о возрождении кыргызского великодержавия.

Пока соседние страны прозябали в варварстве, деспотии и вражде друг к другу, что свойственно всем глупым и авторитарным режимам, в царстве света и знаний Чигу стали проявляться самые высокие стандарты народовластия и справедливости, проходили относительно честные выборы, процветала свободы слова. Страна стала называться островом свободы и даже новой Атлантидой, то есть еще одним совершенным царством древней демократии и справедливости и процветания, что существовала где-то далеко на Запале. И именно на эту страну, царство света и гармонии, равнялись теперь жители Чигу. Это конечно было далеко от правды, но тем не менее, была доля правды в таких утверждения.

Поскольку Бабашбек был очень богатым человеком, ему не составило труда стать сначала депутатом айыл окмоту, а потом и быть избранным в Жогорку Кенеш страны Чигу по партийным спискам.

Короче Бабашбек Жолборсмазаров стал депутатом Древнекыргызского парламента, вследствие чего был вынужден переехать на постоянное место жительства в город Бурану, что в Чуйской долине, которая была столицей царства.

А потом удача и богатство и новые возможности и вовсе вознесли его на самый вверх по карьерной лестнице. Он стал президентом страны Древний Кыргыз.

Надо сказать, что в те времена Бурана, столица государства Кыргыз была большим процветающим городом, и нравы в те времена были примерно такими же, как и теперь, ведь человек мало меняется со временем. Бабашбек стал президентом страны, а его супруга, хотя и была по природе блондинкой и не была похожа на типичных кыргызок - ни в древности, ни в современности, - тем не менее, очень плохо изъяснялась на языке горожан. Поэтому к ним чванливые горожане относились как к мыркам, поскольку оба плохо умели говорить на городском языке, и говорили только по-кыргызски.

Но Бабашбек Жолборсмазарович приложил массу усилий для того, чтобы выучить городской язык, а также стремился всегда ходить в наутюженных брюках и чистой одежде, чтобы не выдавать в себе провинциала.

К слову сказать, Русалка как истинная кыргызская жена, не вмешивалась в дела мужа, даже когда он стал депутатом Жогорку Кенеша, а потом и президентом страны, никогда не поучала своего супруга, не требовала от него дорогих нарядов, зарубежных счетов в банках древнего Гелветистана, Лютеции, Рима или Бейджина.

И Бабашбек Жолборсмазарович возгордился. Он посчитал себя великим политиком и человеком, хотя, в действительности, во всех его достижениях, удачах и успехах была заслуга Океана, его благословителя и тестя.

В один из дней, когда Бабашбек собрался со своими однопартийцами он все—таки был вынужден пригласить свою жену на собрание, посвященное обсуждению очень важного государственного вопроса. Несмотря на то, что Русалка противилась изо всех сил, Бабашбек настоял на своем. А надо сказать, на этом Курултае обсуждался вопрос о том, как сделать страну еще богаче. Депутаты поставили вопрос ребром - как сократить расходы на праздники, тои, похороны и прочие торжественные мероприятия, которые издревле досаждали кыргызов. Дело в том, что кыргызы еще в древние времена отличались чрезмерной расточительностью в этом плане. Если для других народов хватало всего-навсего зарезать овцу, чтобы провести свадьбу или какой-то другой обряд, то у кыргызов было принято как минимум резать корову или кобылу. Эту традицию критиковали много раз, но никак не решались принимать какие-то ограничительные законы. Как только ставился вопрос о снижении уровня поедания мяса, так тут среди чигунцев находились ярые сторонники демократии, которые с пеной у рта доказывали, что это будет нарушением прав человека, что надо резать как можно больше скотины, чтобы хорошо жить и процветать. В результате, собрание, посвященное экономии народных средства и защите естественных богатств и природы, поскольку леса и пастбища также страдали из-за чрезмерного обилия пасущихся на них крупного и мелкого скота, пришло к прямо противоположным выводам. Депутаты порешили не принимать никаких мер и все оставить по—прежнему, и пусть народ сам решает — резать ему или нет скотину по праздникам.

После этого президент и депутаты вместе со своими женами собрались в зале для торжеств, где их ждал торжественный обед, приготовленный в лучших кыргызских традициях. Столы просто ломились от яств и изысканных мясных угощений, там были не только баранина, но и казы-карта, конская колбаса, не говоря уже об алкогольных напитках — короче говоря, кампания против обжорства и излишества, обернулась новыми излишествами и обжорствами. А один из депутатов, кто обладал несколькими сотнями лошадей и тысячами овец даже сострил вместе с очередным тостом, произнеся следующую фразу:

Чтобы спасти наши благодатные пастбища от эрозии
и леса от уничтожения,
надо как можно чаще резать и есть скотину,
чем легче будет нашим пастбищам.

И вот в момент, когда один из депутатов ЖК говорил пламенные речи о том, как прекрасна страна, в которой они живут, Русалка начала судорожно смеяться.

- Ты что жена, твою мать? – разозлился Бабашбек Жолборсмазарович. – Как можно смеяться в такой обстановке? Ты посмотри, какие уважаемые люди здесь собрались?

Но Русалка не могла стразу остановиться, это был не смех уже, а конвульсии, хотя она и пыталась как можно быстрее унять нервический смех и спазмы. Бабашбек был явно не в духе в тот вечер, и ему его прекрасная жена показалась не просто глупой, но и невоспитанной и некультурной мыркианкой, и он ударил ее по щеке.

Русалка перестала смеяться, из ее глаз потекли слезы, и она так сказала своему мужу:

- Вот ты поднял первый раз на меня руки, без всякого на то основания. А если хочешь знать причину моего смеха, то я тебе скажу, что не надо была начинать борьбу с излишествами, если все завершится тем же самым.

Бабашбек Жолборсмазарович испугался от таких слов жены, потому что сильно любил ее, хотя был неотесанным болваном. Он тут же попросил прощения у нее и пообещал, что больше никогда не ударит ее. Более того он тут же подписал постановление о том, чтобы ни один мужчина в его царстве не смел поднимать руки на женщину, зная о том, что точно такой же закон существует и в Атлантиде.

После этого Бабашбек старался не показываться на людях, в общественных местах вместе с женой.

Но трудно предсказать и предвидеть то, что ожидает нас в этой жизни. Несмотря на неисчислимые богатства страны Кыргыз, его по-прежнему не хватало на всех. И это не удивительно. Кыргызы были невероятно праздным и растратным народом. Богатства, которые попадали им в руки, быстро уходило от них, потому что они проводили бесконечные праздники, юбилеи, тои и похоронные процедуры.

А надо сказать, что завистливый и хитрый царь Северной империи, который занимался только тем, что планировал захваты чужих земель, хотя у самого их было более чем достаточно, давно уже положил глаз на страну Кыргыз, видя, каким не прагматичным и наивным является его народ.

Так вот этот царь, подкупая депутатов и правительственных чиновников, стал постепенно скупать стратегические ресурсы этой страны. Таким образом, страна постепенно стали распродавать горные реки, пастбища, дороги, леса, пахотные земли.

В конце концов, дело дошло до того, что депутаты Жогорку Кенеша поставили вопрос о продаже озера Иссык-Куль, чтобы отдать все долги и кредиты, которые все они нахватали в банках у хитрого северного императора.

Депутаты стали проводить одну кампанию за другой, чтобы доказывать простым чигунцам, что только передав Иссык-Куль в собственность другому более могущественному и богатому государству, страна станет по-настоящему независимым и сильным государством. Так сказал Бабашбек и это показали по всем информационным каналам, которые существовали в то время.

Русалка была в гостях у родных и друзей вместе с Бабашбеком, когда разговор зашел о политике, будь она неладной.

Все началось с того, что там, в гостях был один любопытный молодой человек, который спросил мнения Русалки, относительно продажи Иссык-Куля - и действительно ли, это будет способствовать усилению независимости страны?

Поскольку Русалка, как вы помните, была царской дочерью, она не умела лгать, и сказала прямо, что такой шаг, наоборот, приведет к тому, что страна может лишиться независимости. Этот комментарий попал в СМИ, и вызвал скандал в обществе. Получалось, что президент страны и его жена расходятся в таком важном вопросе.

Взбешенный и одновременно испуганный Бабашбек, потому что он боялся, что царь северной страны узнает об этом, придя домой ударил свою жену по щеке. Однако он при этом забыл, кто является отцом его жены, недовольство и гнев которого могли бы иметь куда более катастрофические последствия для него и его страны, чем недовольство северного императора.

- Вот ты ударил меня во второй раз, вместо того, чтобы быть благодарным мне, - сказала ему жена. На этот раз она не уронила с глаз ни одной слезинки. – Помни, что если ты еще раз поднимешь руки на меня, то потеряешь вовек. А что касается продажи Иссык-Куля, никогда не делай этого, если не хочешь, не только потерять страну, но и вызвать гнев Океана.

После этих слов Бабашбек Жолборсмазарович быстро пришел в себя, пал на колени перед женой и стал умолять ее о прощении, обещая, что больше никогда даже не подумает о том, чтобы поднять на нее руки.

Чтобы далее не искушать судьбу, Бабашбек стал даже подумывать о том, чтобы досрочно оставить президентское кресло и отойди совсем от большой политики, чтобы не потерять свою любимую жену, которую он обожал всем своим сердцем полудикого кыргыза и арийца. Да к тому же, уходя в отставку, он понимал, что вопрос с передачей Иссык-Куля в концессию другому государству будет уже приниматься не им.

Однако он не успел этого сделать. В один из дней на берегу Иссык–Куля собрался очередной саммит глав стран региона, которые избрали чисто азиатский путь развития и политического устройства. Это когда цари и президенты однажды избираемые на свою должность или сами себя назначаемые в этом качестве путем войн и переворотов, оставались там до самой смерти или до очередной революции и народного бунта, который бы их смел с насиженного места. Увы, царь Кыргызов тоже попал в эту ловушку клептократов-правителей и начал принимать их идеологию, хотя это в корне противоречило основам арийской цивилизации, чтобы правители правили до самой смерти и при этом нещадно разворовывали страну.

В общем, мероприятие длилось три дня. Главы региона три дня обсуждали, как организовать Таможенный Союз, при этом император Северной державы все обустроил так, что Таможенный Союз якобы способствовал независимости каждой входящей в него страны и подъему его экономики. Хотя на самом деле было ясно и дураку, что из идеи создания Союза вороватых президентов не может получиться ничего хорошего в принципе.

Тем не менее, Бабашбек как царь небольшой страны должен был играть роль гостеприимного хозяина.

И вот в конце этого саммита была культурная часть, где была поставлена пьеса древнекыргызскоо драматурга, которая была признана образцом патриотизма.

В пьесе главную роль играла народная артистка страны Кыргыз, спектакль был посвящен 20-летнему юбилею независимости страны. Но все - и режиссер, и актриса любили не свободную страну Кыргыз, а Караханидский СССР, и не скрывали своих пристрастий, они полагали, что пока не будет восстановлена огромная империя, не может быть речи о достижении подлинной независимости.

Актриса Амал Дейдикматова в самом кульминационном моменте представления воскликнула "Какую страну просрали", произнеся эту речь на языке северной империи, чтобы там оценили, как она любит и предана идее возрождения нового обновленного караханидского СССР

В этот самый момент Русалка принялась смеяться, прямо в зале театра, где она сидела со своим мужем и другими президентами.

- Что это за безкультурье? – возмутился Бабашбек. – как тебе не стыдно, вести себя так по-дикарски в таком обществе. И ударил ее по лицу.

В тот же момент Русалка перестала смеяться и сказала своему мужу:

- Вот ты ударил в третий раз меня, без всякого на то основания, вместо того, чтобы вознаградит меня за сказанные мной слова. Потому что на мне нет никакой вины. Ты потерял меня теперь навсегда. А если хочешь знать причину моего смеха, то я скажу тебе. Только свободный человек может оценить свободу. Эти же артисты, постановщики пьесы и автор спектакля думали совсем о других вещах, их интересовала не свободы, а рабство, они были преданы всей душой ему. Вот над чем я смеялась так горько в день посвященный юбилею свободы вашего народа.

Ну что же, теперь пойдем на берег озера, пришло время расставания. Я покину тебя, но с тобой останутся наши дети, позаботься о них, и они позаботятся о тебе впоследствии.

Вот так они вернулись на берег озера. Бабашбек Жолборсмазарович, как ни умолял свою жену по дороге, чтобы она не покидала его, как не падал перед ней на колени, заверяя ее, что любит ее бесконечно и что больше никогда-никогда не обидит ее, все было бесполезно.

Подойдя к берегу озера Русалка крикнула:

- Ну-ка мои хорошие буренки, овечки, лошадки! Пришло время возвращаться домой! Пошли, пошли, пошли! Кай гут! Кай гут! Кай гут!

На этот зов дружно откликнулись стада коров, овец, косяки лошадей, спускаясь с горных пастбищ к побережью озера. Если прежде их было всего 20 овец, 30 коров, 40 лошадей, то теперь их было в десятки раз больше числом.

Когда Русалка пошла навстречу воде, и стала погружаться в озеро, все эти животные пошли за ней и один за другим исчезли в глубине воды

Бабашбек Жолборсмазарович остался на берегу, обливаясь горькими слезами. Но его скотина тоже несметно размножилась за совместные годы проживания с Русалкой, его овцы, кобылы и коровы скрестились с теми породистыми животными, что вышди из воды и стали многочисленными и породистыми. В общем, сколько скота ушло в воду, столько же оставалось и на берегу - в собственности у Бабашбека. Грех было жаловаться, имея такое богатство. Вдобавок ко всему у него оставались дети - его сыновья, которые росли умными и отзывчивыми и глубоко преданными отцу. Они заботились о нем и ухаживали за ним, глубоко сопереживая его горю. Все они удачно женились, приведя в дом хороших невесток, одна умнее другой, которые также умножили радость и счастье Бабашбека.

Однако Бабашбек был безутешен. В один из дней он пошел на берег озера, и с тех пор его уже никто не видел больше. В народе гоаорят, что он ушел вслед за своей возлюбленной, бросился в озеро.

Говорят еще также, что знаменитое землетрясение, имевшее место 3 тысячи лет в Иссык-Кульской котловине произошло именно по причине гнева царя Океана Кол Буудан-Ата, вследствие чего огромная глыба скалы обрушилась и перегородила Боомское ущелье, и вода затопила большую часть Иссык-Кульской котловины, и многие села и города древнего Чигу скрылись навсегда под водой.

Мы не знаем точно, что было на самом деле, но факт остается фактом, могущественное государство ариев прекратило свое существование, народы, выжившие после этой катастрофы разбрелись по всему свету, исключая горных арией, которые продолжают жить и по сей день, но уже не в том качестве, как их великие предки, равнявшие свою страну в Атлантидой.

Кыргыз балыктардын дастаны

Ысык-Көлдө адам баласы тааныбаган замандан бери Чабак менен Асман балыктары жашап келе жатышкан. Ала-Тоонун жергесинде бир дагы адам тукуму жок болгондо да, ал турсун дүйнө-жүзүндө адам али жарала элек мезгилде да бул балыктар Исык-Көлүбүздүн койнунда ойногон, сансыз көбөюп мындан сулуу, артык, сонун жашоонун сурабай-каалабай, жыргап, чардашкан. Бул балыктын эки түрү Ала-Тоонун накта тамырлаш, түпкү тургундарынан болушат: алар ушул жерден пайда болгон, өсүшкөн, көбөюшкөн, өнүгүшкөн, тарай турган жагына тарашкан. Ошондуктан Асман Борбордук Азиянын, Кытайдын, Афганистандын Кыргызстан менен чектеш тоолуу сууларында жолугат, кыскасы, кыргыздар каерде бар болсо, ошол жерде алар дагы - Чабак менен Асман бар, ал эми Ысык-Көлдүн Чон жана Кичи Чабагы ушул жерден башка эч жерде жолукпаган өзүнчө эндемик урууларынан болушат.

Бул эки балыктын тең этинини таттулугун айтпай эле коелу, алар дүйнөдөгү эң ширин жана таза (асманлай таза жана Ысык-Көлдөй берешен) балыктардын катарына киришет.

Экөө тең балыктардын арасындагы эң момун, пакиза, адамгерчиликтүү, койдун оозунан чөп үзүп жебеген тиши жок, а бирок чабандардыкындай муруту бар балыктардан болушат.

Жашаган суусу бир аз кирденип калса эле ооруй башташат. Жеген азыгы да негизинен Ысык-Көлдүн астында жана суунун үстүңкү катмарында калкып өскөн түрдүү өсүмдүктөрү болуп кыпындай дагы жыртыч касиеттери болгон эмес жана андай болушу да мүмкүн эмес. (Бул жагынан алганда, алар, албетте, кыргыздардан айырмаланган, анткени биз момун болсок да эт жешти кадимки жырткычтардай абдан жакшы көрөт эмеспизби).

Асман балыгынын тоо сууларын бойлой бийик аска-тоолого чыкмай адаты бар, ошондуктан бул абдан назик, тоонун суусундай таза балык Кыргызстандын бардык жайыттарынын сууларында жолугат. Чабандар менен кошо сууну бойлоп, форель жетпеген жерлерге жетип, мөңгүнүн муз аралаш суусун ичип, ийри-буйру тар бирок терең суулардын койнунда шумдуктай ирделип жетилет. Накта жайлоонун балыгы десе болот бул жаныбарды, ал турсун өңүнөн да бул муруттуу, томолок жүздүү жоош жандык бир карасаң, арийне курсак салып жетилген экземплярлары, кыргыздын, чабандын өңүнө абыдан окшошуп кетишет, катигүн, аки-чүкү, алас-булас, көтү-баш - таш ээ, кызыталак. Ал эми Чабак Ысык-Көлдө жашоого абдан көнүккөн суу жаныбары болот. Суу астындагы жайыттарында кадимкидей оттойт. Кыргыз деңизинин асты өзүнчө кооз жана бай дүйнө, сууга чөккөн тоолуу өрөөн, уникалдуу жай, чексиз бир экосистема эмеспи. Анын суу каткан койнунда, күндүн нуру жетип-жетпеген түпкүрүндө Чон Чабак менен Кичи Чабактын өзүнчө жаздоолору, жайлоолору, күздөөлөрү жана терең кеткен кыштоолору бар. Кыштын ызгардуу мезгии келери менен чабак көлдүн тереңдигине көчүп, суу астындагы 100-200 метр, андан да терең чөлкөмдөрдө уруу урууга бөлүнүп кыштайт. Жаз, андан соң жай келери менен суук тереңдиктен жогоруу тарапка, өсүмдүк жайнаган ареалдарга, камыш, чий, чычырканак каптап өскөн жээктерге жакындай баштайт, ошол жердеги күндүн нурунан жылууланган сууларда ири икрасын тууйт, көбөйөт, семирет. Чычырканактын кычкыл-таттуу уругун абдан жактырат, чабак үчүн бул өсүмдүк деликатестин деликатеси болгонун, балык улоочулар (кайырмакка ошол урукту тизип, чабакты тутандар) жакшы билишет. Күз мезгилинде жайы менен семирген балык, жээктен бир аз ыраак жана тереңирээк жайгашып, Ысык-Көлгө куюлган тоолуу суулардын агымдарына ыктаган күздөөлөрдү ээлеп кыштын камын көрө баштайт.

Бир дагы башка суу жандыгы үчүн Ысык-Көлдүн шарты, климаты, суу үстүндөгү жана суу астындагы калкып жашаган флорасы менен фаунасы, топографиясы (деңиз астынынын картасы, өзгөчөлүктөрү, ландшафттары) мынчалык ыңгайлуу болгон эмес. Кыргыздар Ала-Тоодо пайда болгонго чейин миңдеген жылдар илгери эле милиондогон сандагы чабак менен асман, кийинчерээк аларга кошулган сазан менен маринка балыктары да, көлдүн бардык чөлкөмүн сезон-сезондорго жараша тегиз ээлеген, жайыттан жайыттарга көчүшүп, дүйнөдөгү эң бир таза суунун койнунда кылымдап жашап, семиришкен, мындай бейпил балык үчүн бейиш жашоодо тукумун, уругун тазартышып, асылдандырышып, адамзат үчүн өтө баалуу балыктарга айланышпадыбы.

Ооба, Ысык-Көлдүн Чабагы менен Асманы, ичинде бир дагы кири же уусу жок берекелүү кыргыз балыктары, биз өзүбүз баалабаган чексиз байлыгыбыздын, бейиш өңдүү жергебиздин куту экенин кантип таана алабыз.

Бирок бул кыргыз балыктарынын бейиш заманы XX кылым келерии менен түгөнө баштады.

Ала-Тоонун дарыялары да, касиеттүү Ысык-Көлдүн суулары да кескин түрдө булганып, өзгөрө баштады.

Каяктагы үрөйүү суук жырткычтар, өңү-түсү, кебете-кепшири серт балыктар пайда боло баштады. Чабак менен Асмандын тукуму кырылды, майдаланды, сапатын жогото баштады.

Ал эми жырткычтар өсө баштады көбөйүп, санын көбөйтүп, жаңы заң-мыйзамын Ала-Тоого таңуулап.

Эмнегедир бизге сырттан келгендердин баары эле кыска мөөнөттө карышкыр, жырткычтарга айланып кетишет. Өз жергесинде башта жүдөп-какап, лөлү болуп иттин турмушун көрүшүп жүрүшкөн болсо да, бизге келээри менен бултаңдап, семиришип, күчтүү, ардуу, айбаттуу болуп кетишет. Тетиги Армениянын Севан көлүнөн тинтип бизге көчүп келген чичкак форель да, беш-алты жылдан кийин биздин тиши жок кыргыз балыктарды карсылдатып жеп, семирип, акыры мурдагы өлчөмүнө караганда он эсе чоң, коркунучтуу балык манабына айланып кетпедиби.

- Неге мындай, тай ата? – мектептен келген балакай-чабак тай атасынан сурап калат бир күнү. – Бизге бүгүн эжекебиз мектепте илгери Исык-Көлдө чабак менен асмандан башка балык болбогон деп айтып берди. Бирок кийин жергебизге судак менен форель кошулуп, аягында бизди бийлеп калбадыбы?

- Ээ, балам, бул ачуу чындык, - деп, мурутунун сылады тай атасы. - Биз аларды адамча тосуп чыксак, эмнегедир алар бизге башынан эле айбанча мамиле кылып жатышат. Арал деңизинен алып келинген ала-чапандуу Судак дагы Ысык-Көлдө беш-алты жылда эбейгейсиз семирип, жетилип, чабакты да, асманды да, ал турсун баягы форелди да кыскартып жибербедиби. Не себептен мындай болуп жатат дейсиңби?

Анткени, бейиш өңдүү жерибиз абдан бай, кооз, башынан эле тиши жок, тынч, койдой жоош балыктардын түрлөрүнүнүн жашоосу үчүн абдан ыңгайлуу жаралган экен. Кудайды буйругу ошондой болгон экен эзелтен.

- Анда эмнеге, тай-ата, акыркы заманда баарыбыз кырылып калдык? Сиз айткандай миң-миллион жыл бактылуу жашап Ысык-Көлдө, аягында ушинтип жарткычтарга таланып?
- Ээ, балам, биздин кулк-мүнөзүбүз, жашообуз да соңку мезгилдерге бузула баштаган эле, Суулайман пирибизге жакпай, анын кыжырын кельрип.
- Ал кантип болду?
- Беиште жашаган жергиликтүү калк - чабак менен асман - момун, тиши жок, муруту узун, курсагы чоң болуп, соңку мезгилдерде абдан эле жалкоолукка, кенебестикке, тартипсиздикке берилип кеткен болучу. Иштебей эле тойлоп жүргөнбүз акыркы кылымдарда, окууну, билим-силимди биротоло унуткарып, аны менен кошо сый-урматты жоготуп, акыры жайыттарыбыз түгөнө баштаганда бири-бирибиз менен урушуп-талашып ит эле болбодукпу тиши жок, момун балыктар. Ошондуктан бизге каардаган Суулайман пир менен Көлдүн теңири бизге

сабак болсун үчүн чыныгы жырткычтарды арабызга жиберди.

Ошондуктан жергебиз эзели бейиш болгону менен бүгүнкү кунарсыз бапасыз жашоодо, сырттан келгендердин азабынан бара-бара тим эле жырткычтардын бейишине айланып кетпедиби. Ооба, анын үстүнөн элибизди кулк-мүнөзү, пейили да кенен, жумшак, оор ишке көнбөгөн, жаңы нерсени кабыл алууга кызыкпаган, жайлоодо жатып, кымыз ичип ныксырап жүргөндү эле жактырган кудай берген эл экенбиз да.

- Демек, биз өзүбүз күнөөлүүбүз бүт баарына? – дагы сурады тай атасынан балакай-чабак. – Судак тилинен сабак берген эжекебиз, өзү чабак болсо да бизге судак менен форель балыктарынын маданиятын эле мактап калат эмеспи. Анын айтканына караганда биз мурдагы заманда, Ысык-Көлдө судак менен форель жок болгондо, биздин жашообуз абдан жаман, жапайы, өнүкпөгөн болгон имиш. Бири-бирибиз менен тытышып эле жүргөнбүз дейт, ошондой биздин окуган тарыхый китептерибизде да жазылат. Чабак менен асман балыгы ит-балыктан пайда болгон деп, ал эми форель менен судак балыктары байыртадан асыл тукумдуу балыктардан болушуп, Ысык Көлгө келери менен биздин турмушубуз оңоло баштаган экен, балыктардын коммунизми курулуп.
- Бокту жептир ал эжекең - кыжырданып сүйлөдү баласына тай атасы. - Бизди маданиятка, жашоого үйрөтпөй эле кырып коюшпадыбы, жерибизди,

жайыттарыбызды, сууларыбызды тартуулап. Эң аягында, чабак менен асманды саны кескин түрдө кыскара баштаганда бул соргоктордуна айыбынан, алар өзүлөрү да азайды. Анткени бүт барын жеп түгөтүшпөдүбү.

Негизи Исык-Көл жаратылышынан асман менен чабактын жашоосуна абдан ыңгайлуу көл болот. Бул суу жырткычтарды батыра албай табиятынан. Акыры, балам, бары-бир асман менен чабак балыгы Ысык Көлдү мурдагыдай ээлеп калат, жарткычтар менен митаамдар болсо бул ыйык көлдөн толугу менен жоготулат.

- Аны үчүн эмне кылуу керек?
- Биз жыркычтарды жеңишибиз абзел. Конкуренция, атандаштык, эрегишүү деген бизде болгон эмес. Мына ошондуктан башка жерден келген жүдөмүш, итим бай, алдым-жуттум, саткынбайлар бат эле чоңоюп, өсүп кетишет.

Ошоудктан өзүбүздүн жергебизге чындап ээ бололук десек, ошол башкалар менен атандашып иштейли, күрөшөлү, изденели, мээнеттенели. Алар байыса, мейли, байысын, бирок биз алардан артта калбайлы. Мына ошондо мекенибизде жырткыч, митаам, жексур, сүткөр, ара-тумшук, балка-тумшук, балта жутар, чоймо оз, шапалак, чыйылдак балыктары, ар-түрдүү былыктар жоголуп, акыры баардыгы тең жана бактылуу бири-бирин чындап урматтам, ызаттап жашап калышат ко деймин.

Демек сен дагы балам, өзүңө окшогон чабак менен асманга дос бол, алардын тилинде сүйлө, алар менен бирге иште, алардын кызыкчылыгын корго. Форель менен судактарга жакын жолобо, алар сенин өлүмүңдү гана эңсешет. Манкурт болуп калган чебак менен асмандардан да этият бол, алар менен достошконун жакшыга алып келбейт. Себеби алар арак ичишип, ойноп жыргап, форель балыгынын ургачы сойкуларынын торуна илинишип, акыры жок болушат.

А сен болсо башынан таза жана пакиза жашоого берилгин, көп окуу жана көп өнөрлөрдү үйрөнгүн, эне тилиңди, байыркы тарыхыңды терең үйрөн, сырттан келген митаамдардын тилине жана тарыхына алданбагын.

- Форель менен судактардын баардыгы эле жаман эмес да?
- Албетте, тукуму жыркычтардын арасынан да жакшылары, боору-керлери бар. Алар менен жакшы болууга аракет кыл, алардын мыкты сапаттарын үйрөнүүгө далалат кыл, бирок айтып коеюн сага, тилиң менен дилиңди аларга эч убакта сатпагын.

Эң оболу таза сууга, таза жашоого, таза сүйүүгө, таза билимге, таза ишенимге дайым умтулгун биздин улуу ата-бабаларыбыздай, аз уктап көп иштегин, изденгин, чыдамкай, эр-жүрөк болгун, Суунун пиринен, Көлдүн теңиринен жардамды, кеңешти, кечиримди сурап тургун чарчабай-таалыкпай. Ошондо акыры соноюн ирделип жырткычтарды да жеңе турган абалга жетесин.

Эртели-кечпи, балам, Ысык-Көл мурдагы бейиш абалына кайра келет жана бул ыйык көлдү жалаң гана тынчтыкты сүйгөн жаныбарлар ээлеп калат. Ошондуктан, бүгүн биздин жашообузду жырткычтар менен митаамдар башкарып жатса да, алар баардыгы кырылып жок болушат же, эгерде биз менен түбөлүк жашагысы келсе, биздин байыркы тилибизди, салтыбызды, жашоо өнөрүбүздү үйрөнүүгө, терең урматоо аргасыз болушат.

Бул Ысык-Көл деген бейиштин көлүнө Жараткандын койгон эзелки жана түбөлүк талабы, заң-зүңү болот. Аны бузгандын баары кырылып жок болот, муну эсиңе бекем туткун, кайрадан ыйык жериңе ээлик кылайын десең.

THE EPILOG

Life without gratitude

No matter how much
blessed people
by Heaven, Evolution
or something else
still unknown to Mankind
as universal Casino astonishing -
they are all leave so arrogant
and so disgraceful
for the small piece of nasty stars ashes
so lucky and marvelously arisen
from absolutely nothingness
after billions years
of enormously fights, waiting and preparedness.

Don't worry and complain
or cynically schadenfreude
upon great mystery of our reality,
very soon
coming time for return
even if you won Jack Pot
you will disintegrated, dissipated and forgot

as one dust grain among million trillions
never born to this life so enthralling and trilling.

http://www.igetoo.com/montres/eleanor-rigby-the-chronicles-of-great-love-and-fall-of-great-empire-english-edition-/1_7pktu-B00L8IUWZG_1

The loophole of rescue

Our expanding universe
where we born 3.7 billion years
and matured,
after another billion years
turned from cradle of life
to the Death prison
when world collapsed
for the total destruction.

But human civilization
have a chance
to avoid such awful self-crashing
if we learn to sneak out
through loophole
to another universe

But it would be extremely
difficult task,
said physicist Michio Kaku,
demanding from future generations
the great technologies
and lot of Energy and compassion.

But how about
save our country right now
from strong pulling of Cleptocratic Federation
which unite and join by corruption,
bribing, fearing elite and heavy agitation
the weak post-soviet states and nations
that going unavoidable
to the total distraction?

Where and how, my love,
we find or create loophole
leading off from the Deadly universe of fatal degradation
toward the really freedom and restoration?

Kyrgyzstan in the first years of its political independence had a great opportunities for creating a completely new society based on social justice, laws and democracy and for gaining enormous success which would exclusively valuable not only for our nation but for future and prosperity of whole Central Asia.

At the early 1990 all the freedom world and their dozen and even hundred international institutions turned to help us and support our proclaimed democratic reforms – technically and financially.

Even the simple fact of opening foreign states embassies in the capital of Kyrgyz Republic and transforming our main airport "Manas" to international gate had a great political, economical and psychological influences for our nation and establishing its identity.

But if we added the decent fact that western countries (USA, West Europe and Japan) seriously believed for the intention of our first president Askar Akaev and decided really help to him to creating the aisle of Democracy in Central Asia, you must assess and measure the exceptionally lucky historical chance that blessed all of us in that past decades - from 1990 till the 2000 and even more till the 2005.and even now we don't lost all hope but our presidents and governors can't have done anything with the devastative corruption and personal irresistible desire and lust for grabbling and stealing billions from own people and their future - and run out from country when coming the next revolution.

It might be said the best what we have had mentally, genetically and politically set to battle with the worst part of our nature and traditional police and West trying to keep our best way and paid for that but this intentions had to do with the strong and highly efficient oppositions and propaganda of Kremlin politics together with massive export of corruption going to fail all of our initiation for the creating new society.

What it happened is the classic example of failed dream when one had a lack of strong belief. We just simple underestimated the power and nature of really freedom and democracy and preferred again returned to comfort of slavery.

Act of creation

God seems created this enormous universe
from one point and emptiness
as if after tragic lost his best beloved,
whom he so treasured and limitless devoted,
that after shocking acknowledging her vanishing,
So greatly hated the Death
that decided to wipe it away and nothingness at all
from own kingdom and unfolded shape of existence
expelled them jealously and mercilessly
from any spaces, measures and universes
and ways of life - possible and non-possible
have left any small room at all
for mundane, mortality, mediocre and misery,
presenting in honor of great love
for her memory, commemoration and unavoidable resurrection
this stunned act of creation
with greatness in macro and micro
on the countless grades and levels
and quantum-limitless unfolded and unraveled energy,
matters, thoughts, dreams, imagines and eternity.

http://www.amazon.in/s/ref=nb_sb_noss_1?url=search-alias%3Dstripbooks&field-keywords=Partridge+singapore

The loves serenade from Orozkul accompanied by the Komuz of String Theory

I have lived and fallen in love with all 50 billion females
that ever had come in our planet
and with other 50 billion that will come in a future
and they all deeply loved me
and left wonderful remembrances and marks in my heart
and I surround by eternal love and filled with great energy
flown reviving trough a dying universes

And no one man and husband and hero of jealosity
no despite and hate and pursue vindictively me
because all this women were mine.
Yes, I married and had precious honey month
not only with Kok Sulu and Sharon Stone
but with Egyptian Cleopatra and queen of England
in the time of Shakespeare and much later,
and with queen and first ladies from XXY century,
especially queen Diana and great singer Anna German
from XIX adored me
and I them but I was extraordinarily happy with all women
even with ambitious and stubborn as Margaret Thatcher and miss
Reagan
and I find harmony with unworkable wife of Abraham Lincoln
and with all bitches in mediaeval and modern Asia and Europe
and save them from punishment and flame
and with great number of grethen, maragaret, aysha, aisuluu and
others best beloved
completely hidden in various times and parts of world and unknown
but found by me as far galactic through Hobble telescope.

How it would be possible you asked me?
I answered my heart have been just a decent mathematic
and used precise equation
for catching the loves wavering of every one of them
with the exact probability and expectation.

You said - it was unbelievable,
they are all had own fate, dear men, families.

Sure, but all it were the tiny parts of their realities:
Everyone according with law of Quantum physic
and hidden protocol of Dark matter matrix
have a multiple realities and transcendences.
Мы живем во множестве реальностей и явлений.

My soul just accounted and created formula
for find out, calibrate and increase the most favorite projection
from every woman who ever lived in Earth
who was built to deep love and attraction to me.
Мой душа просто вычислила и сотворила формулу
поиска, калибрации и реализации моей собственной проекции,
в которой каждая женщина, жившая когда-либо на Земле,
была обречена и сотворена любить меня
самой глубокой и преданной любовью.
Мы живем в бесконечном множестве вселенных
но любовь помогла мне
разрешить величайшую загадку вселенной.
И я сотворил мир моей совершенной любви и вселенной.
Я полюбил каждую женщину на этой планете
и они меня полюбили
и провела со мной лучшие годы жизни

и никто не был обесчещен и обманут,
ни одни мужчина не был в претензии ко мне,
что мне удалось сорвать все звезды на небе,
которые прнадлежали по праву мне.
We are all living in multiple universes.
yet don't guess about it at all
but love unraveled this riddle
and helped me to sneak out to precious goal.

That's way I am reopen this marvelous unlimited reality
find way to mystery of every living creatures
and I loved all of them and made amazing acquaints
and created marvelous choices, heaven blessed unions.

And what's more I penetrated much more further,
to find way for hearts and love of all dear women,
that never was born and rise from primarily status
but whose quantity so great outnumbered
the sands grains of Sahara desert
replicated billion times.
Yes I found out so many loves and worlds
that I decided to create the giant ark of love
filled and tightly packed with my innumerous favorites
and once these treasures postulated own universes,
the ark boarded to new reality
with such rules, laws, matters and structured spaces
where I find place for resurrection and eternal life
to all the hearts who potentially able to love me
and I might love them in my multitudes.

Thus born the string theory of Universe
precisely tuned for goddess love
originated from one heart
but tuned as sophisticated trap
for all beauties absolutely catching and saving up
by that very ambitious and jealous chap.

And he now pretty understood
how lord loves us and waits long
for our respect and gratitude.